# DESIGNS
## FOR
## FOREIGN LANGUAGE TEACHER EDUCATION

Newbury House Series

# INNOVATIONS IN FOREIGN LANGUAGE EDUCATION
Howard B. Altman, Series Editor

*Individualizing Foreign Language Instruction:*
*Proceedings of the Stanford Conference*
Howard B. Altman and Robert L. Politzer, Editors

*Individualizing the Foreign Language Classroom:*
*Perspectives for Teachers*
Howard B. Altman, Editor

*Speaking in Many Tongues:*
*Essays in Foreign-Language Teaching*
Expanded 2d Edition
Wilga M. Rivers

*Changing Patterns in Foreign Language Programs:*
*Report of the Illinois Conference on Foreign Languages*
*in Junior and Community Colleges, 1972*
Wilga M. Rivers, Louise H. Allen, Sandra J. Savignon,
Richard T. Scanlan, Editors

*Individualized Foreign Language Learning:*
*An Organic Process*
Gerald E. Logan

*Performing with Objectives*
Florence Steiner

*Designs for Foreign Language Teacher Education*
Alan Garfinkel and Stanley Hamilton, Editors,
Bonnie Busse, Lee E. Hawkins, Genelle Morain, Renée S. Disick,
Robert Morrey, Jean-Pierre Berwald and Manuel Pacheco

*Creativity in the Language Classroom*
Irene E. Stanislawczyk and Symond Yavener

*Learner-Centered Language Teaching*
Anthony Papalia

# Designs
## for
## Foreign Language Teacher Education

*Editors*

Alan Garfinkel
*Purdue University*

Stanley Hamilton
*Bridgewater (Ma.) State College*

*NEWBURY HOUSE PUBLISHERS, INC.* / *ROWLEY* / *MA.*

**Library of Congress Cataloging in Publication Data**

Main entry under title:

Designs for foreign language teacher education.

(Innovations in foreign language education)
Bibliography: p.
Includes index.
1. Language and languages–Study and teaching--
United States. 2. Teachers, Training of--United
States. I. Garfinkel, Alan. II. Hamilton,
Stanley. III. Title.
P53.D4   418'.007'1173      76-20755
ISBN 0-88377-062-8

*Cover design by Kathe Harvey*

NEWBURY HOUSE PUBLISHERS, Inc.

Language Science
Language Teaching
Language Learning

68 Middle Road, Rowley, Massachusetts 01969

Printed in the U.S.A.                    First printing: November 1976
                                              5   4   3   2   1

*Bonnie B. Busse* (Ph.D., The Ohio State University), Associate Professor of Spanish at Northeastern Illinois University in Chicago, Illinois.

She has had years of experience as a Spanish teacher and currently is responsible for Spanish teacher education at Northeastern Illinois.

*Lee E. Hawkins* (Ph.D., Indiana University), Director of Language Arts Instruction, Niles East High School, Skokie, Illinois.

He has taught French at the junior and senior high levels. He formerly taught a methods course for French teachers at the University of Illinois. He has contributed to *The Modern Language Journal* and *The ACTFL Review of Foreign Language Education, Volume 4.*

*Genelle Morain* (Ph.D., The Ohio State University), Associate Professor of Foreign Language Education at the University of Georgia.

Her articles have appeared in *Foreign Language Annals* and in Volume III of *The Britannica Review of Foreign Language Education.*

*Renée S. Disick* (M.A.T., Stanford University), teacher of French at Valley Stream Central High School, New York.

She has long participated in programs for in-service teacher training. She is the author of *Individualizing Language Instruction: Strategies and Methods* (Harcourt Brace Jovanovich, 1975), the co-author with Rebecca Valette of *Modern Language Performance Objectives and Individualization* (Harcourt Brace Jovanovich, 1972), and has written for *Foreign Language Annals, The French Review* and *The Modern Language Journal* among others.

*Robert A. Morrey* (Ph.D., Stanford University), teacher of German at Cupertino (California) High School.

He has contributed articles to *The Modern Language Journal* and to other Newbury House volumes.

# Contributors

*Jean-Pierre Berwald* (Ph.D., The Ohio State University), responsible for the training of graduate assistants in the Department of French and Italian at the University of Massachusetts at Amherst.

His articles have appeared in *The Modern Language Journal* and in *American Foreign Language Teacher.*

*Manuel T. Pacheco* (Ph.D., The Ohio State University), Dean of the Laredo Campus of Texas Agricultural and Industrial University.

He formerly taught at the University of Colorado and Florida State University, and has contributed to *The Britannica Review of Foreign Language Education,* Volume III.

*Stanley Hamilton* (Ph.D., University of Michigan), Assistant Professor of Foreign Languages at Bridgewater State College (Mass.).

He has taught methods and French courses at Purdue University, University of Michigan, and Wittenburg University, and his articles and reviews have appeared in *The French Review* and *The Modern Language Journal.*

*Alan Garfinkel* (Ph.D., The Ohio State University), Associate Professor of Modern Languages and Education at Purdue University.

He has contributed to *Hispania, The Modern Language Journal,* and Volume III of *The Britannica Review of Foreign Language Education.*

As editors, we owe the strengths of this volume to our collaborating writers. Their painstaking work and innovative thinking have made the book a reality. Our work has been to organize the text, bringing its separate parts together. Blame for any shortcomings must therefore be laid at only our doors.

Special gratitude is due to our families and friends who have helped us at every stage in the preparation of this book. Howard B. Altman went far beyond the requirements of a Series Editor to assist us, and we thank Sonya Garfinkel for her sharp eyes, sharper blue pencil, and support.

We hope this text will contribute to the professional education of prospective foreign language teachers, and we invite readers to send us their reactions to the ideas expressed here.

A. G.
S. H.

# Acknowledgments

# Contents

Approximately 1200 colleges and universities are authorized by state departments of education to prepare prospective foreign language teachers for certification. Although there are various plans of study, programs share common features.* Nearly all the programs, for instance, require some preparation in methods of teaching. Sometimes this training takes the form of a general course intended for all prospective teachers, regardless of the subject they intend to teach. Other schools provide a specialized course for those who intend to teach foreign languages; certain fortunate institutions offer separate methods courses for each language.

A foreign language methods course has the potential for making some vitally important differences in teacher preparation. Without such a course, there are two likely alternatives: (1) to send the prospective teacher out for his or her student teaching after a general methods course with no specific preparation in foreign language methodology (one wonders how many student teachers then would be able to break the cycle of teaching as they were taught). (2) The prospective teacher would be apprenticed to a certified teacher for a period of time. The probable result would be a faithful copy of one teacher or another, with little influence if any from the profession at large. This book focuses on the foreign language methods course and the purposes it alone can accomplish in the education of prospective foreign language teachers.

The foreign language methods course provides a unique opportunity to observe a wide variety of teaching and learning styles. The teaching ability of the instructor often provides a model. In addition, because of the university's central

---

*Ryan, Kevin (ed.), 1975, *Teacher Education, The Seventy-fourth Yearbook of the National Society for the Study of Education, Part II.* Chicago: National Society for the Study of Education.

Introduction

location and its extensive audio-visual resources, students can benefit from filmed, videotaped, and live observations of large numbers of successful foreign language classroom teachers at work. The foreign language methods course also gives students a forum to explore, discuss, and evaluate the specific literature of language pedagogy. It can orient the student to periodicals and reference works normally available in campus libraries.

Such a course has the additional advantage of gathering students with similar interests in a common pursuit. Fullest advantage is made of this like-mindedness when methods students are exposed either to the textbooks they will use in teaching or to similar ones, and collaborate on writing specific exercises and lesson plans to be tried out when they teach. In this way, prospective teachers can be guided in defining the roles that such things as psychological principles will play in their careers. Further, simply getting to know other prospective language teachers who are at the same stage of preparation can prove to be a cornerstone for the building of professional relationships that may favorably affect subsequent teaching.

Finally, the teaching of foreign languages usually involves fewer, more clearly delineated goals than do, for example, the teaching of English or Social Studies, some of the affective goals notwithstanding. Because of this narrower focus, every prospective teacher should expect to be trained in specific, widely accepted practices. As well, perhaps the greatest strength of the methods course is to foster self-esteem and confidence that follow when a teacher has a plan of goals for the students, while stimulating a healthy attitude toward self-analysis and the need for continual refinement of methodological practices.

Each contributor to this volume has attempted to be as specific as possible about how methods instructors should direct students in achieving certain competencies. Competency is taken to imply both *knowledge* and *ability to perform.* There is a compelling reason for this emphasis on competency. It is closely related to recent calls for teacher accountability. Teachers are being asked, in a sense, to guarantee that students who pass their courses will have a specific, demonstrable ability to perform in accordance with course objectives. Before long, this guarantee may even be the subject of judicial proceedings. In some cases, the new emphasis on competence originates from the profession; in others (the state of Texas, for example) the movement has been mandated by law. Whether courts uphold these laws or not, the foreseeable future appears to promise continued and vigorous emphasis on what prospective teachers can be expected to *do,* possibly because, in the past, the foreign language teacher has promised too much with insufficiently precise statements of goals.

This work is addressed to prospective methods instructors—either those with specialties in other areas or those in graduate programs of foreign language education—who contemplate their first methods course. The order of the printed chapters does not imply any given format for the methods course. Likewise, the bibliography does not attempt to be exhaustive.

Eight separate topics have been chosen for inclusion in this volume. Six were selected because they treat procedures representative of those demanded by the profession of any language teacher. Such professional demands logically should influence the scope and content of the methods course. That may seem to be a tautology; but anyone familiar with the realities of the situation will agree that these professional demands are reflected in too few methods courses today. The remaining two chapters were chosen because they treat specialized topics in methods instruction. Although they are not necessarily experienced by all prospective language teachers, the same kinds of professional demands that call for the inclusion of the other topics also influenced their selection.

Listening and reading, the receptive skills, are the subjects of Chapter 1. Little justification is needed for the methodologist's treatment of universally recognized parts of all comprehensive language courses, but it is important to note that neither skill can be treated lightly or peripherally. If there ever was a time when listening was treated as a skill to be developed only incidentally, and the chief procedure in the teaching of reading was the physical act of handing a student a book, that time is past. Teachers now are called upon to examine the foreign language content of a class session to assure themselves that they provide quite specifically for auditory discrimination and comprehension. Further, they are asked to provide an analytic approach to reading that makes available to the foreign language student the same array of contextual and morphological aids to reading he "exploited" when he was learning to read his native language. Thus, the receptive skills deserve thorough study to help the prospective teacher satisfy these new demands.

Similarly, the generative skills are subject to new roles as integral elements of the comprehensive language course. Teachers are being called upon to do more than simply prepare students to speak. They are required to provide real opportunities to use the foreign language in situations for which pattern drills were never intended to suffice. They are also asked to give students the same opportunities to personalize their writing in a foreign language. Chapter 2 presents the ways in which the methods course can assist prospective teachers in meeting those requirements.

Chapter 3 deals with the teaching of culture and a promise to familiarize students with a foreign culture often made by teachers but not always kept. Lorraine A. Strasheim* has reminded us of the fact that few teachers neglect to mention the "cultural values" of learning a second language while equally few make special provision in their instructional programs for knowledge of the cultural environment of the language they teach. Morain suggests and illustrates some specific ways for prospective teachers to be taught to provide that familiarity more efficiently than they otherwise might.

---

*Keynote address, January 1974. Northwest Indiana Foreign Language Teachers Association, La Porte, Indiana.

Chapter 4 also is concerned with teachers' commitments to students. It is focused on today's requirement for teachers to be committed to affective education. This calls for concern for how students *feel* as well as for what they *know* and *do* in a language class. Now that the added dimension of how students feel has been analyzed and implemented, we need to discuss the reasons for including affective education and the specific procedures that can be employed. Disick makes a strong case for careful consideration of the affective education movement by prospective language teachers in their methods classes.

Individualized instruction in foreign languages has also received the kind of attention in the language teaching field that demands a place for it in the methods course plan of study. Individualized programs of diverse designs remain constructive and welcome elements in today's pluralistic language teaching. In Chapter 5, Morrey discusses advantages and disadvantages of individualization and offers practical information on implementation.

Two specialized areas of language teaching methodology are the topics of Chapters 6 and 7.

In Chapter 6 Berwald describes the special training needed by graduate teaching assistants to teach their basic courses. The forms for this specialized area are illustrated by models for graduate-assistant training.

In Chapter 7, Pacheco discusses the special training of teachers of those whose native language is not English. The sociological issues involved include the new emphasis on ethnicity now apparent in what was thought to be the American "melting pot." This emphasis calls for special attention to bilingual and bicultural education. Pacheco outlines the sociological issues and provides annotated references to information on this specialized aspect of teacher education.

Chapter 8 of this volume is a bibliographical review of foreign language education. The methods class teacher is provided with sources of information to aid those who feel they should go beyond the scope of this volume in planning their courses.

Collected at the end of the book are references related to each of the chapters of the book.

Our overall purpose here has been to make concrete suggestions for methods instructors to choose from in designing their methods courses according to their goals *and* in conjunction with the needs, interests and capabilities of their students.

Alan Garfinkel
Stanley Hamilton

## INTRODUCTION

Convenience and general agreement dictate that reading and listening be considered as receptive skills (Jarvis, 1970). The nomenclature "receptive skills" in no way implies a passive or nonproductive learner; rather, the name merely emphasizes that receptive skills are not manifested visibly or audibly. Professional literature suggests that reading and listening rely on comparable cognitive abilities which enable the learner to decode linguistic symbols, whether auditory or visual. Phillips recognizes the teacher's function in the learning of reading skills by treating reading as problem-solving behavior (Phillips, 1975). So, reading and listening tasks are grouped because each requires abilities to decode and reconstruct received messages. Similarly, speaking and writing are grouped because they require the ability to encode. Today's casual observers and language teaching specialists of some years ago have grouped visually oriented skills (reading and writing) with aural-oral skills (listening and speaking). However, close examination of the nature of the work called for in mastering each skill has led contemporary authorities to change this grouping. Mueller (1974) exemplifies this pairing of listening and reading in a most cogent treatment. My examination of these skills and what is taught about them in the methods course will employ the same kind

1

# Listening, Reading,
# and the Methods Course

5

*BONNIE B. BUSSE*

of structural plan that I recommend for organizing the methods course. This plan calls for *discussion, observation* and *participation.*

The *discussion* segment focuses upon identifying characteristics of the skills. It may take the form of lecture, or it may involve methods students more directly than a lecture can by requiring them to make at least some of their own generalizations about the nature of the skills presented.

The *observation* segment calls for more active involvement than does a lecture. Here, methods students examine teaching materials and (wherever possible) teaching itself in order to select and identify specifically designated kinds of techniques.

The *participation* segment gives the methods student the opportunity to try his hand at teaching for the first time. Here he presents a short lesson of perhaps five minutes' duration. The methods teacher makes notes on a score sheet which lists characteristics that he wants his students' first teaching work to display (Politzer, 1966; Politzer and Bartley, 1967). Students see the sheet before teaching and, in fact, may even make notes for one another to determine the degree to which each lesson taught displays those characteristics. Language students for the lessons may be fellow methods students, volunteers from basic language courses or, in the best of all possible worlds, real students from high school study halls. This kind of participation is often called "microteaching" and much has been written about it by generalists (Allen and Ryan, 1969) and by specialists (Politzer, 1966; Politzer and Bartley, 1967). Let us examine, then, specific ways for the methods teacher to treat the receptive skills—listening and reading—with this three-part structural plan.

### Teaching listening skills: Discussion

Ideally the ultimate goal in listening comprehension is the ability to understand native conversation at normal speed in uncontrived situations. A shorter term goal aims toward an understanding of the target language as used by native or quasi-native speakers in situations appropriate to the interests and proficiency of the foreign language learner (Starr et al., 1960). Controlled listening exercises by means of experimental tools from human communications research may facilitate the identification of short- and long-term goals (Huberman and Medish, 1974). The student who listens to a second language with any degree of success has learned to function on two levels described by Rivers (1968). The same author further explicates listening comprehension by using edited and unedited texts (Rivers, 1975a; 1975b).

Rivers' first or "recognition" level includes the development of an ability to discriminate the phonemes of the target language and to perceive distinctive elements of pitch and intonation. Also involved at this level is the perception of structural interrelationships among the various components of spoken utterances—recognition of tense clues, person, number, *actor* and *acted upon,* as well as other syntactically or morphologically determined features of sentence structures.

At the second or "selection" level, Rivers describes the student as having so thoroughly internalized the grammatical features of typical utterances that he can now focus on the semantic aspect of the phrases. If communication is the goal of language instruction, the teaching of comprehension is essential at both levels. It is obvious that without it communication does not exist. Few textbooks, however, concentrate on sequential development of the listening skill beyond the earliest stages of instruction. While some programs offer exercises for sound discrimination, not enough provide a variety of taped listening comprehension selections. This is the reason it becomes especially important to sensitize methods students to attend to the listening skill. It is always wise to question methods students as to the purposes of their listening comprehension exercises—do they aim at that elusive objective, understanding, long before elementary decisions as to tense, number, context and register have been established? Ample time in the methods class should be devoted to observing different kinds of exercises to develop appropriate problem-solving abilities.

### Teaching listening skills: Observation

Sound discrimination exercises and simple listening comprehension drills constitute basic approaches to the listening skill that methods students should observe and identify. Minimal pair exercises form the cornerstone of the listening skill in many commercial texts of the audio-lingual and post-audio-lingual era. At the opposite end of the curriculum, students might demonstrate their ability to identify regional speech; intermediate goals might concentrate on materials of a progressively less contrived nature. Methods students will profitably consult Valette and Disick (1972, ch. 8) for their discussion of performance objectives that pertain to listening comprehension. A six-step approach underlies their proposed sequential development of the listening skill: (1) perception; (2) recognition; (3) reception; (4) communication comprehension; (5) criticism; (6) evaluation. Rivers (1968) identifies possible instructional strategies for these six steps, from which I cite two examples.

*Elementary level—stage three*: Prepare true-false questions for the student to hear after he listens to variations of dialogues or reading texts previously covered. Or, these same items might be transformed into visual props, sketches perhaps, which the student identifies as true or false according to the passage he hears.

*Intermediate level—stage two*: Relate an amusing incident which took place on the way to school; start the class with some interesting or timely news items or narrate a dramatic reading written in conversational style. These activities could be teacher-led or student-led.

(Note that these examples of stages two and three are limited to the listening skill; they do not mix skills, with the exception of the student's performance in the intermediate level example.)

The parts of the methods course devoted to observation should enable the methods student to select and identify listening exercises which range from minimal pair drills to pure or mixed-skill listening comprehension exercises. Students can do this by reporting on textbooks they have examined and by giving reports on the work of unnamed teachers they have observed. This can be facilitated by asking students to secure permission to visit the classes of teachers they may know, making teacher-to-teacher arrangements for such visits or making videotape recordings in various classrooms. Once able to select and identify kinds of listening exercises, methods students should be encouraged to start planning for their first teaching experience.

## Teaching listening skills: Participation

A methods student's first experience in teaching listening is likely to take the form of a short lesson of perhaps five minutes' duration. The student may teach his lesson to peers, to first year college students or even to high school students in a high school building. The methods teacher lists the characteristics he wants each teaching session to display (e.g., audiovisual devices to assure comprehension) and shares that list with the class. Steiner (1975) provides step-by-step guidelines in developing listening comprehension, from the beginning to advanced levels, which might well be incorporated into the checklist. With the checklist available to the entire class, improvement becomes a common goal and self-examination a routine matter. Here are examples of some techniques that methods students might employ during this stage of the methods course.

The first involves commercial materials that are frequently available from textbook salesmen; methods students prepare a small unit based on such material, with adequate advance preparation of language students in three ways: what is to be learned, how it is to be learned and the purpose of the learning, and how the students are to be evaluated. For listening exercises extracted from unfamiliar material, new vocabulary and structure must be explained if they are not readily understandable on the basis of context.

The second technique, the audio-motor unit (Elkins, Kalivoda, and Morain, 1972; Kalivoda, Morain, and Elkins, 1971) provides listening practice by supplying language learners with a taped series of related commands to which they listen as the teacher carries out the commands in pantomime. The teacher then asks the class to act out the commands as they hear the tape replayed. Methods students can prepare tapes in advance.

A third effort to enhance listening ability promotes the use of magnetic boards and flannelboards, both of which permit the visuals to be used in a variety of configurations. Students are called to the board and given instructions in the foreign language to rearrange the visuals on the board. Visuals are prepared during the methods class.

A fourth technique adopts paper-and-pencil scoring by training students to be alert to structural signals by listening to a series of sentences in which students signal the presence or absence of a certain feature, for example, the subjunctive. This type of exercise is purely aural, in that the response is a mere checkmark.

Fifth, films can be made into valuable listening comprehension exercises even if their sound tracks are not appropriate for a beginning language class, because new sound tracks for the film can often be supplied by recording a tape to be played in conjunction with the film. Often the short 8-mm films used in other disciplines to teach a simple concept (the economic law of supply and demand, for example) can be utilized with language teaching sound tracks in this manner. Undergraduate curricula libraries often own collections of such films which methods students can adapt and borrow later during their student teaching.

A sixth technique assumes that the radio is an effective classroom medium for listening comprehension. Future teachers might prepare material to be used in conjunction with the radio or they might produce a radio program for a specific purpose. Short-wave broadcasts in the target language are an inexpensive source for some timely new listening material. If short-wave equipment is not available, a nearby university might record the broadcast over the telephone; free program notes are sometimes published in both English and the foreign language for domestic programs aimed at sizable ethnic populations. The following is an example of a student-produced Spanish variety show format (Garfinkel, 1972).

1.  Announcer gives a monologue followed by guided response questions.

2.  Proverbs are presented with meaningful sound effects and context in order to facilitate comprehension.

3.  Commercials (some chosen because their English versions would be familiar) are used repeatedly and supplemented with guided response drills.

4.  Other components might include musical interludes, jokes, tongue twisters, interviews and weather reports.

Finally, student teachers will need to practice writing tests to fit listening objectives. Examples (such as ABCD tests in which the learner chooses a letter as a rejoinder to a pictorial stimulus) may be presented on dittoed sheets or on the overhead projector (Valette, 1969; 1967).

### Teaching reading skills: Discussion

The task of the learner in learning to read a foreign language shares aspects with the task of the learner whose goal is the spoken language, in that the learner reacts to a message which comes from an external source. The medium of the message is different and face-to-face contact is absent; the beginning reader has the advantage that he can control most often to some extent the rate at which the message is transmitted to him. This may seem obvious, but it should be pointed out to methods students because it is the basis for a recent change of emphasis in the discussion of reading. Wardhaugh (1974) offers an informative account of the relationship between linguistics and reading which methods students may profitably consult. To illustrate that the topic of reading continues to receive imaginative and provocative attention, students may consider Twadell (1974) and Jarvis (1973).

Discussion might begin with two possible definitions: (1) reading is the pronunciation of phrases and sentences of written symbols; (2) reading is the following of written sequences rapidly for comprehension, usually performed silently while the eye scans whole groups or words or sentences at a time (Michel, 1967). Prospective foreign language teachers might observe several notes of caution concerning these definitions. Traditionally, reading has meant reading *aloud*, but reading aloud was rarely conceived as speech and the notion of communication with another person (the listener) went largely unnoticed. Also, reading aloud was paired with oral translation, most often prepared on the basis of word-to-word dictionary homework, itself the fruit of misleading principles of dictionary usage.

While we might concur that oral reading and concomitant control of sound/symbol correspondence are appropriate to early stages of foreign language training, teachers have turned since the mid-1960s to silent reading for comprehension as their main reading objective.

### Teaching reading skills: Observation

In observing the teaching of reading, the student teacher must be able to identify the principal techniques for teaching reading comprehension at varying levels of difficulty. Scherer (1963) has furnished a system for classifying reading comprehension tasks which re-oriented the teaching of reading in the mid-1960s. According to Scherer, the student learns to read as much as possible by direct association between the printed target language and its meaning. The spoken foreign language serves as intermediary. While Scherer perceived the goal as total comprehension ("liberated reading") without recourse to English, the prospective teacher must know how to set realistic intermediate goals with respect to local curriculum objectives. Essential to the realization of any long-range goals are these guidelines:

1. Reading begins with language to which students have listened.

2. New words are introduced with careful spacing to minimize reading "stoppages," and marginal glosses are furnished.

3. New words are re-entered as soon and as often as possible.

4. Structure is kept at a level the student is accustomed to, or is learning to control.

5. The student is urged to use both grammatical clues and pragmatic contextual clues to narrow the possible or probable meanings of words.

6. The student is encouraged to tolerate a certain degree of temporary vagueness while developing skill in sensible guessing.

7. Cognates and derivational systems are fully explained and exploited in instruction.

8. Evaluation is provided at every stage.
   Scherer (1963).

Methods students may be asked to examine text materials and to make reports on classroom observations and videotapes of classroom teaching in order to test their ability to classify reading exercises. The Scherer system might be used or the classes of reading exercises explicated by Valette (1969), Valette and Disick (1972) and Steiner (1975). Six stages of reading development have been thoroughly treated in recent publications by Rivers (1975a, 1975b).

## Teaching reading skills: Participation

Student teachers need to practice administering a number of devices for the teaching of reading before a group of language learners. Short lessons are used in much the same way that short lessons are used for teaching listening skills; these suggestions will incorporate recent innovations.

Techniques that stress the sound-symbol relationship begin the reading sequence. The teacher prints words from a dialogue the student can comprehend aurally on large cards. The words are printed on cards of different colors. After reading practice under the teacher's guidance, the students are asked to arrange the cards in the proper order. Then the sentence is reread and students are asked to replace a word (card) with another word having the same function. Then the sentence is read. This process is repeated for each sentence that has been drilled in the preceding oral-aural stage.

Techniques involving paraphrasing are also useful. The most difficult words in a reading selection are underlined on a duplicated copy of the selection. Simplified glosses of the underlined words are recorded on a tape which accompanies the reading passage on an otherwise word-to-word basis. Language learners read the written selection and are moved along in their reading according to the pace of the tape.

Students must also be taught to make inferences with regard to the meaning of unknown words. Allen and Valette (1972) list suitable techniques. Attention must be given to clues such as the degree to which new target language words match or fail to match the native language in meaning. Similar comparisons can be made to discover false cognates, cognates which have common spellings and/or pronunciations. Other clues include prefixes, suffixes, predictable spelling changes, word families, compound words and the context of new words. Student teachers should realize that their students rarely have the wide vocabulary they assume necessary for making inferences and contextual assumptions; Phillips (1975) provides practical guidelines.

The CLOZE technique provides another device that student teachers might use. Here words are removed from a printed passage and students use surrounding words and thematic context to supply missing words (Culhane, 1970). One experiment used a CLOZE passage to measure proficiency in English as a Second Language; a 234-word passage had fifty blanks to be filled in thirty minutes. When scored twice (once for *exact* responses and once for *contextually acceptable* responses) the CLOZE test supplied information on English as a Second Language proficiency and served as a useful diagnostic tool (Stubbs and Tucker, 1974).

Student teachers must have practice in devising reading materials toward which their students are likely to have a favorable psychological set. Seelye and Day (1971) demonstrate the use of newspapers in the preparation of contemporary reading materials, a task which language students themselves could assume for their classmates' use. Another device which receives increased attention is the bilingual column reader which enables students to use native language skills. Jakobovits (1968) and Parent and Belasco (1970) support intelligent use of the native language in learning to read a foreign language.

**CONCLUSIONS**

This approach to the receptive skills attempts to involve prospective teachers in at least three kinds of methodological preparation: *discussion* based on recent research, theoretical issues and standard techniques, *observation* devoted to the identification of those standard techniques in a sequential instructional process and *participation* which employs teacher-made materials for teaching and testing purposes. Practical suggestions for teaching receptive skills to foreign language students, and methodological preparation for prospective foreign language teachers who expect to teach the receptive skills have spanned a number of alternatives and approaches.

Earlier in this chapter the relationships between the two receptive skills were set forth. A further comment now in order is that reading materials were and often are derived from prior listening comprehension materials. Although the audio-lingual method today dictates less and less of our professional thinking, one holdover from the 1960s merits our reconsideration: the listening → reading sequence. While reasons for retaining this sequence may vary, its soundness is largely uncontested by most foreign language teachers.

My practical suggestions for foreign language teachers are necessarily the result of my own experience and biases. It is, of course, the methods teacher's duty to provide specific suggestions without turning them into ultimata. Beginning methods teachers are advised to enumerate, consider and evaluate whatever preconceptions they bring to the methods class. I want my suggestions to be approaches for a variety of actual foreign language programs designed to meet individual and curricular needs in both self-paced and traditional programs in the receptive skills. The foreign language methods instructor hopefully will find a start toward his teaching of the receptive skills—both in the area of talking about them and in the actual student teacher-centered classroom practice.

NOTE. References for this chapter, and all other chapters, will be found at the end of the book.

## INTRODUCTION

Speaking and writing are generative skills which demand that the second language learner master the skill of encoding language symbols for others to listen to or read. Because they are readily observed when practiced they are the most frequently noticed of the language skills. People commonly make note of the languages one speaks or writes, but they are seldom quite so aware of those one can read or listen to. So, the attention commonly given the generative skills and their indispensable roles as intrinsic elements of communication dictate that the methods course devote a significant portion of its time allotment to the teaching and testing of these skills.

In Chapter 1, Busse has proposed a three part organizational structure for dealing with the receptive skills. Her plan applies equally well to the generative skills and I have employed it here to emphasize the fact that generative and receptive skills complement each other as elements of communication. Busse calls attention to *discussion, observation* and *participation* in organizing the methods course. *Discussion* gives methods students an opportunity to learn something of the nature of the skills. *Observation* allows them to see different strategies in use and *participation* involves them in actually teaching short lessons of limited scope

**2**

# Speaking, Writing, and the Methods Course

15

*LEE E. HAWKINS*

to a small group of language learners. I will examine both of the generative skills separately here in terms of each of the three parts of Busse's organizational plan.

### Teaching speaking: Discussion

The babbling infant spends many hours learning his home language. The babble is interpreted by some observers as meaningless prattle, by others as reasoned hypothesizing about the surrounding language. At some given point the infant learns that his noises cause people to respond differentially to varying utterances; satisfaction of needs relates intimately to verbal behavior, although there is disagreement as to the nature and development of this relation. Until the mid-1960s, theoreticians urged foreign language teachers to imitate home language learning in foreign language teaching. Flaxman (1961), Ausubel (1964), and McKay (1960) expressed reservations about this view, although the leaders of the foreign language teaching profession felt that a child could most economically learn a second language if it were taught in a manner similar to the way he learned his home language. These home circumstances are not necessarily the most favorable, however; Lenneberg (1964) observed that a youngster learns the home language under the most adverse conditions. An ideal school setting could therefore possibly even improve upon the prevalent home conditions. In practical terms, nonetheless, the school cannot re-create the conditions of infancy where the socio-psychological need to communicate is imperative. Later, the older foreign language student demonstrates a different, perhaps negative, attitude toward language learning that studies of motivation continue to examine.

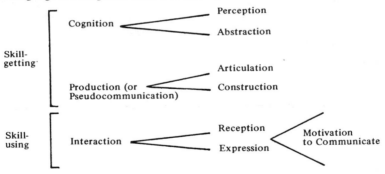

**Figure 2-1**    Rivers' model of language learning (from *Speaking in Many Tongues,* Newbury House, 1972 and 1976).

Rivers (1972) has provided us with a discussion of the nature of language learning which is especially useful to methods teachers and students because it can be readily applied to the very things they do or have done to master language skills themselves. Rivers' description includes all the basic skills. It employs Parker's terminology (1970) to focus on two major aspects of language learning called "skill-getting" and "skill-using." To paraphrase Rivers, cognition, the formation of one's mental blueprint which leads one from a model of language to language production, takes place as new language symbols are perceived and abstracted. "Skill-getting" is completed when articulation and construction based on cognition form production or pseudocommunication. "Skill-using," Rivers continues, is predicated upon motivation to communicate. That motivation leads to reception, expression and interaction or communication (Figure 2-1).

In applying the Rivers model to a discussion of the speaking skill, the methods teacher should emphasize the role of perception and abstraction in the formation of the language learner's plan for action (cognition). It is even more important to stress the need to distinguish between "skill-getting" and "skill-using" and further to note that no real ability to communicate results from work at "skill-getting" alone.

## Teaching speaking: Observation

The methods course should provide an opportunity for students to examine the work of practicing teachers and an assortment of materials intended to develop the speaking skill. Some practicing teachers may allow videotapes of their classes to be made for this purpose. Others may permit student teachers to visit classes. Since the methods teacher better serves his university by being personally acquainted with most of the teachers in the local community, it is advisable for him to make arrangements for such visits and tapings.

The observation of teaching and teaching materials should require prospective teachers to do two things. First, student teachers need to determine the objective or purpose of whatever they observe. Second, they should classify the teaching or materials they observe to get some idea of where they fit in the learning process. Students might employ the Rivers model here in order to make their involvement with it more active than passive.

By determining objectives of the procedures they observe, methods students can get a vivid illustration of the value of setting clear objectives. On occasion, they will observe things which have no apparent objective. Such a paradox can make that illustration even more impressive.

Classifying procedures in terms of a model of learning leads the methods student to ask vital questions about the nature of the teaching and materials he has observed. For example, if the methods student reads a textbook which provides materials for "skill-getting," but not for "skill-using," the Rivers model can intensify his awareness of this problem and lead him to set more demanding criteria for any text he may later use.

## Teaching speaking: Participation

Participation in short teaching experiences is the next task the methods student faces. Emphasis should be on building communicative ability, but methods students must also know how to administer brief drills if needed in establishing the readiness provided by Rivers' "skill-getting" stage. Stack (1973) names and classifies most such drills. The methods student should get some practice with these drills. They are especially useful whenever a highly structured "warm-up" period seems necessary. But they should never replace techniques like the ones mentioned below. Drills, after all, fail to provide the essential element of communication, the need to speak. Methods students and language learners faced with too many drills rightfully ask:

    a. Why talk about an uninteresting topic?

    b. Why talk about an uninteresting topic in a foreign language?

Hawkins (1972) advocates the identification of student interests and the creation of related materials. One longitudinal study of student interest (Lowry and Reilly, 1970) revealed that money, sex adjustment and health were among the topics most frequently on students' minds in 1919, 1935, and 1957. Future teachers should develop dialogue materials around similar topics and carry out preliminary testing on methods class peers. A benefit from this procedure is that native speakers of the target language will resemble more closely the classroom foreign language learners—they get angry, they get flustered, embarrassed and they stumble even in a "foreign" language! Another benefit accrues from student talk: the foreign language teacher is thereby silenced.

In working with exercises designed to go beyond the pseudocommunication stage, such as the exercises I describe here, some foreign language teachers prefer to stay completely on the sidelines. I encourage student teachers to correct only those errors which interfere with communication. Habitual and noisy correction relates to reduced student talk; a simple restatement by the teacher seems a wise tactic (Damoiseau, 1969).

Besides the informal oral warm-up, the dramatization of skits furnishes relatively spontaneous (but structured) oral practice during which the student teacher can pay special attention to pronunciation, intonation and gesture. Any corrections that the teacher may make are as much for dramatic purposes as any other.

A third device uses a repertory of numbered file cards, each with a question or command in the target language; at the beginning of the class each student receives four or five. When class routine begins to lag, the teacher takes a brief moment to call out a number, whereupon the appropriate student reads his file card. Teacher-talk is reduced to "numéro quatre" and the student responds with the question on his card indicating "number four." This device allows the students to serve both as initiators and respondents in the conversation according to preset conditions.

Oral skills receive further attention in Savignon's (1972) description of a colleague's visit to the foreign language classroom to perform routine gestures—sitting down, opening a book, looking at his watch. Students then recount orally what they have observed. The perhaps unfamiliar person stirs their concentration via the involuntary attention that Belyayev (1964) portrays as an avenue to the more stable conscious voluntary attention. A native speaker might attract involuntary attention in the same way in order to induce students to converse with an unfamiliar pleasant individual. Methods instructors should suggest a list of questions that prospective teachers might use to help their students stimulate conversation.

Joiner (1974) suggests another procedure which prospective teachers might employ. Language learners are encouraged to complete such tasks as guessing a number from one to fifty that the teacher has in mind. She notes similar things can be done with birthdays, prices, and nouns within certain logical classes.

Catalogs, whether in English or the target language, can easily motivate communication. If they are in English, a bilingual dictionary will be needed. If not, a monolingual one will enhance communicative ability. Language learners are asked to peruse the catalog and make a target-language list of things they want. They can then tell what they want and ask others to do so with only a minimal amount of help which the student teacher can supply with an overhead visual that lists basic structures.

Language teachers who work in areas served by a branch of American Telephone and Telegraph Company (Bell Telephone) will find that many of the materials dealing with native language communication provided by that company can be used in second language classes. The company loans devices that simulate live telephone conversations, films, and booklets which list procedures for classroom communications games.

Future teachers may indeed prize oral skills as the road to meeting student interest; yet the assessment of oral skills often lacks meaningful relation to conversational fluency. In evaluating oral skills, methods students must understand that there are relationships between linguistic and communicative competences, although we do not know the precise nature of those relationships. We do know, however, that attempts to communicate a real message, in whatever grammatical form, must occasionally take precedence over attempts to perfect a student's command of grammar (Rivers, 1972).

Longstreet's concept of academic ethnicity (n.d.) attunes the student to what is really important, and in our case, students soon realize that oral skills receive shallow treatment on tests—and they proceed to study what they expect to be tested on. Rivers (1968) observes that students downgrade the importance of an activity if it is not reflected in the final grade. Ease of scoring notwithstanding, oral tests demand our future teachers' urgent attention (Valette, 1967).

### Teaching writing: Discussion

The methods instructor should give future teachers detailed recommendations on how to teach the writing skill. The methods course might consider to what extent the development of the writing skill begins with training in the reading skill. Chapter 1 in this volume notes the preeminence of sound-symbol association in the student's ability to move from the visual stimuli to the acoustic product as he reads aloud. Writing, too, calls perhaps on the student's ability to read silently (or to read aloud) as he writes. One has only to observe a student copying out a written exercise to surmise how he reads to himself as he writes. Many professionals feel that the writing issue varies from one foreign language to another, to the degree that the orthographic system "fits" the phonological system of the target language. Some audio-lingual proponents reflected this viewpoint in recommending that presentation of the written language follow, at some interval, listening and speaking practice of a given passage. On the other hand, advocates of more immediate presentation of the written equivalent point to the fact that many students invent their own spelling systems in an attempt to "preserve" the text they are hearing. Common sense supports the earlier introduction of the graphic system to bypass this often deleterious habit that beginning foreign language students cultivate.

The methods instructor could formulate a prefatory statement to methods students on the development of the writing skill. What might this statement include? Writing seems to be crucial to almost any traditional "method" of teaching foreign languages, and particularly to testing and measurement of foreign language skills. Writing demands that the student *read,* or perhaps *see,* what he is writing; and we have already commented that many students *pronounce* what they are in the process of writing. Dictation takes learning into another sense modality, with the requirement that the student transcribe what he *hears.* If we accept the validity of each of these statements (and they derive largely from common-sense observation), then we have laid the groundwork for supposing that proficiency in the writing skill varies as a function of the development of the component skills—listening, speaking and reading. Thus, even though one may plan to deal with only one skill, the interrelatedness of language skills will force instructional strategies to involve other skills.

### Teaching writing: Observation

The methods student who observes teaching and materials designed to enhance the writing skill faces the same tasks he had in observing techniques to be used with speaking. First, he should examine the purpose and objectives of the teaching and teaching materials he observes. Second, he should classify those techniques and materials in terms of a model of learning. Rivers' model (Figure 2-1) will enable students to discriminate between items that fit logically into a sequence of learning and those that do not. This will enhance methods students' ability to select materials and methods.

### Teaching writing: Participation

Now the methods instructor can proceed to practice some commonly employed techniques for the teaching of writing. I will begin with the use of a three-stage *copying* exercise: (a) pronounce the text; (b) write the text; (c) pronounce the text again. The simplest type of *verbatim* copying, primitive though it may be, presents clear demand on the student's grammatical understanding and attentiveness to overall meaning. In spite of (or perhaps because of) the student's being "given" all he needs in copying, foreign language teachers are surprised to observe many errors in the direct transferral of a text from one page to another. Our visually oriented, billboard society depends more on general visual impression than on the minute identification implicit in the foreign language writing skill.

Although there is by no means unanimity on the soundness of the copying technique, future teachers might evaluate a second type of copying which calls for grammatical changes in the text. Tense change, person shift, and affirmative-negative alternation determine changes in meaning while at the same time requiring concomitant grammatical adjustments.

Free composition, the eventual goal, results from a gradual freeing of the foreign language student from external, mechanical constraints in favor of real expression of idea. Grammar becomes the servant rather than the master of free composition.

Future teachers should prepare a range of writing exercises to span a continuum that might look like this:

word transcription → dictation transcription → verbatim copying →

altered copying → guided composition → free composition

Exercises and devices intended help to bridge the gap between simple copying and free composition are numerous. The methods course should present several and give prospective teachers a chance to prepare them and present them to language learners.

A commonly used device which places stress on word order is the "dehydrated" sentence. The words of a meaningful sentence are taken out of order. All inflected forms are simplified so that a conjugated verb, for example, would be reduced to an infinitive form. Then the language learner is asked to properly readjust the forms and word order.

Labeling pictures of items whose names in the target language are known to the learners is another well known exercise.

Language learners may also be asked to write in words missing from a sentence. In cases where the exercise is too difficult, a list of items from which the correct item may be selected can be used. Much insight is to be gained from studying the same topic through an assortment of tenses, with suitable alternatives in vocabulary and structure according to the achievement level of the students. One obvious consequence of this project is to individualize segments of training in writing—students "cover" the same material (an assigned topic) in exercises appropriate to their level of competence.

Other forms of guiding correct composition include converting dialogues into indirect discourse and providing questions whose answers, if written into a paragraph, form a composition.

Paulston (1972) suggests a form of guided composition which allows a certain amount of choice so that sentences produced by some students will vary from those done by others and still be correct. Each sentence of the composition is written as a separate exercise which requires the student to choose one of several subjects, one of several objects, etc. The new sentence written by the student must make sense. Also, if one sentence allows the choice of "is going to cross the ocean," the student needs to avoid the subsequent choice of "by train" in another sentence of the composition.

## CONCLUSIONS

Attention to the conditions operant during the learning of the home language pointed to an evident focus on the speaking skill and its origins in early childhood. School foreign language learning circumstances rarely incorporate personal and social motivation which foster language onset and development. Personally meaningful topics, however, appear to engage foreign language students in valid speaking practice without undue teacher-dominated emphasis upon impeccable style and pronunciation.

A certain easygoing (not to say carefree) learning atmosphere might do most to encourage the development of the speaking skill, particularly for adolescents whose fear of ridicule teachers must appreciate and understand. A similar atmosphere should contribute to the relaxation of time-honored criteria of grammatical and stylistic correctness which have cramped our foreign language writing exercises. Producing simple prose that conveys a message should be an objective for a fourth-year high school or second-year undergraduate foreign language class.

A comparable gradation of exercises might well serve to guide the development of the speaking skill; the methods class should stress that, whether for speaking or writing, the importance of pacing is paramount. No greater disservice could be rendered to our foreign language students than to allow them to speak or write "freely" without proper preparation for the spontaneous exploitation of the generative skills. Most prospective teachers will encounter the endless corrections of a written composition or the tiring and often futile repetition of a taped "free" conversation.

Prospective teachers should urge foreign language students to pursue their own interests. But our misguided and understandable sense of responsibility for the cultivation of the generative skills must not give way to aimless conversation far beyond the skills of the participants. Structured practice in speaking and writing, with attention to message and form, can allow for spontaneous interchange.

In our zeal to stress the generative skills under the rubric *communicative competence,* we may wrongly retain a traditional allegiance to the written word in the form of priorities on penmanship and "black and white" evidence of learning. Troyanovich (1974) examines the overemphasis of writing in traditional foreign language instruction and concludes that the preoccupation with pencil and paper bears little relationship to foreign language students' psychological and practical needs.

Methods instructors might follow Troyanovich's perspective in reviewing methods class instruction. Do we give added bonus to the future teacher who writes well about theoretical matters of rare immediate import in the foreign language classroom? Does a lot of aimless enthusiastic talk take precedence over informed guided discussion? Are most of our methods projects written? Do we assign grades in foreign language methods class after the methods course itself? Or do we assign grades at the conclusion of the student teaching experience when there has been an opportunity to see the students who actually apply what they learn in the course and those who do not? Does a fine, sound lesson plan mean more than a finely executed sound lesson plan?

It appears that the methods course has a twofold obligation with regard to the generative skills: (a) to portray recent thinking in curriculum and instruction matters relevant to speaking and writing and their applicability to the classroom, and (b) to teach (by example in the methods course) a concept of generative skills that places high priority upon graded activities ranging from controlled exercise to free expression. This progression is the proper domain of the methods course in its treatment of the generative skills.

From the first moment he sets foot in the classroom, the beginning language teacher becomes an "expert" on foreign culture. It makes no difference that his expertise is derived from one college text and four back issues of *Paris Match*; school personnel and townsfolk alike view him as a virtual cultural attaché. Students bombard him with questions about the foreign people and their life style. The Rotarians request an after-dinner speech on international commerce. The PTA needs folk songs for the fall fiesta. By the end of September the "expert in residence" is secretly convinced that he knows very little about the foreign culture, is unsure how to teach what he does know, and is unaware of where to go for further information.

To imply that the foreign language methods course alone provides the solution to this problem would be presumptuous. The methods course can, however, give the future language teacher three things: (1) an understanding of the nature of culture, (2) competency in using specific techniques to teach and test culture, and (3) a knowledge of where to acquire cultural information. This chapter will discuss these areas, present examples of techniques for teaching culture, suggest learning activities for the methods class, and offer bibliographic information.

**3**

# The Cultural Component
# of the Methods Course

25

*GENELLE MORAIN*

# Understanding the nature of culture

*Culture Defined.* What is this "culture" that has become the intellectual responsibility of a language teacher? In recent years, a bipartite definition has evolved. The traditional view of culture ("formal culture" or "culture with a big C") refers to the collective achievements of a people in the arts, in science, in technology, and in politics. The anthropological view of culture ("deep culture" or "culture with a small c") refers to the daily patterns of living as they reflect society's values and cultural assumptions.

This somewhat artificial division in terminology has given rise to an equally artificial division of loyalties. Traditionalists, clutching their literary anthologies, pose rigidly on the "big C" side of the culture fence, while progressivists, armed with social questionnaires and case histories, stand fast for the "small c" approach. In reality, both traditional and anthropological aspects of culture are so interwoven that a valid separation in the language class becomes impossible.

By the time he enters the methods course, the future teacher usually has a reasonable familiarity with the formal aspects of the target culture: its history, its fine arts, and its social institutions. Information of this nature usually is included in a "civilization" course offered by the language department. The future teacher should also have some idea of the social themes, assumptions and value systems which determine the life patterns of those who speak the foreign tongue. Unfortunately, courses designed to impart understandings of this type are not often available to the foreign language major. The methods instructor may find that his course provides the only opportunity to awaken the future teacher to the anthropological aspect of culture.

*Analyzing Cultures.* Prospective teachers need guidance in knowing how to analyze a culture. A helpful analogy might be drawn between the human body and a culture. External characteristics such as pigmentation, hair, height and facial features make men appear differently. Under the epidermis, however, all men share essentially the same skeletal framework, the same organic components. Similarly, even though cultures differ markedly on the surface, there are certain structural constants which provide a supportive framework for any society: the need to obtain food and shelter; the need to relate to others; the need to achieve a sense of personal completeness.

Students should realize that the surface expression of these underlying features is different. As man interacts with his environment, the products and patterns which result form the outward contours of culture. The stranger in a foreign culture comes into contact with these surface contours. When they differ markedly from the external forms of his own culture, his thwarted expectations produce a sense of distress and malaise known as "culture shock." His reactions may run the emotional gamut from timidity to hostility, with a strong sense of revulsion sometimes developing toward the host culture.

Teachers must be aware of the points where there is a discrepancy in cultural fit, where the cultural assumptions of language students differ from those of the speakers of the foreign tongue. Cultural insights illuminating these stress areas should be given first priority in deciding what to teach. Areas where cultural contours tend to harmonize are less likely to lead to misunderstandings.

## Suggested References

Gorden, Raymond L., n.d. *American Guests in Colombian Homes: A Study in Cross-Cultural Communication.* Contract 1-7-070267-3973 between Antioch College as administrative agent of the Latin American Program for the Great Lakes Colleges Association and the U.S. Office of Education.

Hall, Edward T., 1966 (1969). *The Hidden Dimension.* New York: Doubleday, 1966. Anchor Books, 1969 (Paperback).

Hall, Edward T., 1959 (1961). *The Silent Language.* New York: Doubleday, 1959. Fawcett World, 1961 (Paperback).

Lado, Robert, 1957. *Linguistics Across Cultures.* Ann Arbor, Michigan. See Chapter 6, "How to Compare Two Cultures," 110-123.

Ladu, Tora Tuve, 1968. *Teaching for Cross-Cultural Understanding.* Department of Public Instruction, Raleigh, N.C.

Murdock, George P., et al., 1945. *Outline of Cultural Materials.* New Haven, Conn.: Yale University Press.

## Activities for the Methods Class

1. *To understand the framework of culture*: Edward T. Hall (1959), in attempting to define the skeletal outline of culture, lists ten categories which he calls "Primary Message Systems." These cultural constants make up "the map of culture," and include: Interaction, Association, Subsistence, Bisexuality, Territoriality, Temporality, Learning, Play, Defense, and Exploitation.

Divide the class into groups of two or three students and ask each group to formulate its own list of "Primary Message Systems" (cultural constants). Urge them to break away from Hall's list by expanding or contracting categories. When the groups have finished, ask a student to conduct a discussion during which a composite list acceptable to the majority is constructed on the board.

2. *Analyzing one's own culture* ■ ■ *Assignment*: Ask each student to formulate a list of activities relating to life in his home town which, if followed by a foreign guest in that community, would bring the stranger face to face with significant aspects of culture. The following list, submitted by a student from a small rural community in the South illustrates the technique:

### Suggested Activities for a Foreign Visitor

1. About 10:00 a.m. take a coffee break at the Main Street Cafe where the younger businessmen and politicos meet. Note attitudes, deference, evidence of Babbitism, and the informal power structure.

2. Watch the noon quiz shows and soap operas on TV, knowing that most housewives of the town will be doing the same. That night visit the Starlight Drive-In Theater to see what the teenagers are watching.

3. Go to the county high school and have lunch in the cafeteria. Talk to the principal. Note the regulations and punishments imposed on the students. Visit some classes to observe teaching styles. Note interaction among students and teachers.

4. Visit the local Employment Office. See what jobs are available and who is applying for them. Listen to some job interviews.

5. Late Friday afternoon, after paychecks have been collected, go to Foodland or Buy Wise to see how people shop. Do different social classes buy differently?

6. Attend a football game at the high school and note the attitudes of parents, students, and townsfolk toward the home team, the visiting team, and the officials. What role does pageantry play (marching band, drill team, cheerleaders, flag-raising ceremony)?

7. Go to Red Bailey's Barber Shop, preferably early Saturday morning. Listen for examples of typical folk humor.

8. Attend a picnic or cookout at Lake Springs. Note unstructured family relationships, nonauthoritarian attitude of parents.

9. On Sunday morning go to Elvida Richard's Bible Class at the Methodist Church, an interesting example of social, moral, and religious interaction.

10. Visit the maintenance and practice session of the Volunteer Fire Department. Notice teachers, businessmen, and a minister serving under the chief, a journeyman printer.

*In class*: Choose one or two lists and discuss with the class the Primary Message System these activities involve. Divide the class into small groups where each student shares his list. Ask each group to choose an activity from one of the lists and prepare a role-playing skit to illustrate what happens when a foreigner enters a cultural situation which conflicts with his own experience. For example, in the list above, the scene at an Employment Office could provide examples of social attitudes at variance with the stranger's expectations. Have the groups present their skits and follow each with discussion as to how differences in surface contours of culture can lead to culture shock.

### Setting cultural goals

Classroom optimists in the early 1960s vowed to teach their students to speak with "near native fluency." Would this goal also apply to functioning culturally within a foreign environment? Can language students be trained to operate in a culture with "near native fluency"? The realistic response is "no." Only spies in fiction seem to achieve such a goal, and even Super Spy usually has tripped himself up by Chapter Seven. A more reasonable cultural goal is the one expressed at the end of the 1960s: to enable the student to function as a "welcome stranger" in the target culture.

If students are to reach such a goal, it is essential that language teachers do not look upon the study of culture as merely an accumulation of facts. While there are advantages in knowing dates, places, and names associated with the cultural development of a people, more viable aspects of culture must be interwoven with language study.

To function as a "welcome stranger," the language learner should be familiar with the assumptions of the culture and know the accepted patterns of behavior for frequently encountered social situations. He should have some idea as to why this behavior is important and how it relates to other patterns within the culture. He should understand the priorities within the value system of the culture and how these are likely to influence day-to-day behavior.

## Activity for the Methods Class

*Practice in Formulating Cultural Goals.* Discuss briefly with the students the main themes to be found in the target culture. For example, Ladu (1968, *Teaching for Cross Cultural Understanding,* p. 7) lists the following themes from French and Hispanic cultures:

| French | Hispanic |
|---|---|
| L'individualisme | Individualism |
| L'intellectualité | "Regionalismo" |
| L'art de vivre | "Dignidad" |
| Le réalisme | Orientation toward persons |
| Le bon sens | "Serenidad" |
| L'amitié | Beauty |
| L'amour | Leisure and work |
| La famille | Human nature mistrusted |
| La religion | "Cultura y Realidad" |
| La liberté | Rising expectations |
| La justice | |
| La patrie | |

*Assignment*: Ask the students to write five behaviorally oriented goals which involve the language learner in an understanding of cultural themes. Caution them to beware of such vague terms as "to come to know," "to appreciate," and "to gain a feeling for." The goal should be worded to indicate *exactly what the learner will be doing* when he demonstrates that he has met the goal. The following examples could serve to illustrate the assignment:

1. The student will locate an article in a Spanish newspaper which illustrates the theme of "Dignidad" and will explain briefly in Spanish how the reported event relates to this theme.

2. Given free advertisements selected by the teacher from a German magazine, the student will identify the cultural theme or themes represented by each advertisement.

3. After watching a simulation of a French guest leaving a party, the student will identify the theme illustrated and explain briefly in French how the guest's behavior relates to the theme. (The theme of *individualisme* is illustrated by the departing guest's handshake and verbal goodby to each individual guest. The French consider it courteous to devote full attention to one person at a time. Contrast this to the American's exit line, "Well, goodby, everybody," accompanied by an inclusive wave of the hand.)

In class, discuss the cultural objectives written by the students and encourage them to revise faulty or ambiguous items.

## Testing for attainment of cultural goals

Methods students may find it difficult at first to write test items which check understanding of patterns, themes, attitudes, and assumptions. Such an item might ask the learner to draw on his knowledge of cultural patterns to select the correct multiple choice response. Or it might ask him to write a paragraph analyzing a cultural situation drawn from life or literature. The learner might be asked to designate a specified behavior as either "typical" or "nontypical." He might be requested to match pictured gestures with their meanings or tell how best to solve a conflict situation. Sometimes the learner himself might be required to produce appropriate behavior (say and/or do the right thing) in response to a given stimulus.

*Suggested References*

Clark, John L. D., 1972. *Foreign Language Testing: Theory and Practice.* Philadelphia: The Center for Curriculum Development.

Lado, Robert, 1961. *Language Testing: The Construction and Use of Foreign Language Tests.* New York: McGraw-Hill. pp. 275-298.

Nostrand, Frances B., and Howard Lee Nostrand, 1970. "Testing Understanding of the Foreign Culture," in (H. Ned Seelye, ed.) *Perspectives for Teachers of Latin American Culture.* Springfield, Ill.: State Department of Public Instruction. pp. 161-170.

Seelye, H. Ned, 1970. "Performance Objectives for Teaching Cultural Concepts." *Foreign Language Annals 3*: 566-578.

Valette, Rebecca, 1967. *Modern Language Testing: A Handbook.* New York: Harcourt Brace Jovanovich.

*Activities for the Methods Class*

*Writing Items to Test Goal Attainment.* A well written behavioral objective often serves almost word-for-word as a test item. Ask the students to convert the cultural objectives they wrote earlier into test items which will check for attainment of the objectives. Follow with discussion.

*Creating a Performance Test* ■ ■ *Assignment*: Ask the students to devise a performance test which could be used to check attainment of the following objective:

> The student will demonstrate socially acceptable behavior, both verbal and nonverbal, by reacting appropriately in nine out of ten simulated situations drawn from the target culture.

A suggested list of behaviors appropriate in some common social situations—French, German, and Spanish—follows on pages 32-33.

*In class*: Divide the students into small teams and have them take turns administering their tests to each other. Follow with class discussion as to difficulties encountered in formulating test items, rating performance, etc.

### Techniques for teaching culture

In recent years the language teaching profession has developed specific techniques for teaching culture, ranging in complexity from the simple "cultural aside" to the highly organized "culture cluster." Other techniques, such as the programmed culture assimilator packet and the mini-drama, have been introduced from sociology and related disciplines. Methods students should be aware of these techniques, know how to use them for maximum effect, and be able to create their own materials when necessary.

*Creating the Cultural Island.* Perhaps the ideal setting for a language lesson would be a sidewalk cafe on a busy street with the sights, sounds, smells, and flavor of a living culture providing the backdrop. Few motivations are so real as the need to order a good meal, or the furtive desire to eavesdrop on a conversation at the next table. Admitting the impossibility of such a backdrop for most language lessons, the next best thing is to make the learning setting as stimulating as possible.

Too many teachers fail to see the possibilities for dimensional use of a classroom. They change the bulletin board every six weeks and forget that today's student lives with music that vibrates in the marrow, tastes that fizz, colored images that pulsate and glow. Eyes that have seen the far side of the moon will not focus for long on three square feet of static bulletin board. The methods instructor must inspire future teachers to think beyond the three foot frame.

A teacher of French, for example, should be encouraged to take a serious inventory at the beginning of the year: "What is there of France in this room that students can see and touch? What is French here that they can hear? taste? smell?" Consideration for these categories can lead to the development of a "cultural island" in the classroom where students feast their senses on such cultural contacts as the following:

To see:     Advertisements, cartoons, paintings, posters, stamps, street signs, book jackets, maps, charts, sketches, telephone directories, photo-

# CONVENTIONAL PROPRIETIES IN SOCIAL SITUATIONS
(Use as basis for formulating behavior-oriented test items)

S = Statement
R = Response

| Situation | French | German | Spanish |
|---|---|---|---|
| 1. Wish someone a happy birthday. | S. Bon anniversaire.<br>R. Merci. | S. Herzlichen Glückwunsch zum Geburtstag.<br>R. Danke. | S. Feliz cumpleaños.<br>R. Que tengas muchos más. |
| 2. Ask someone to do you a favor. | S. Auriez-vous la bonté de me rendre ce petit service?<br>R. Avec plaisir, Mme. (Mlle.., Monsieur) | S. Kannst du mir bitte einen Gefallen tun?<br>R. Gern. | S. Se lo agradecería si me pudiera asistir en esto.<br>R. Con mucho gusto. |
| 3. A chance encounter with a friend. | S. Quel plaisir de vous rencontrer.<br>R. Qu'est-ce que vous faites là? | S. Es freut mich'dich wiederzusehen. | S. ¡Qué alegría es volverte a ver!<br>R. Ay, ¡cuanto tiempo! ¿Qué cuentas? |
| 4. Complimenting someone on a new dress, hairstyle, etc. | S. Comme votre robe vous va bien.<br>R. C'est une petite robe de rien du tout. | S. Dein neues Kostüm gefällt mir. | S. Qué vestido tan bonito. Está precioso.<br>R. Gracias. Muy amable. |
| 5. Bump into someone and apologize. | S. Pardon. Je vous ai fait mal?<br>R. Non, ça va. Ce n'est rien. | S. Verzeihung! | S. Perdóneme, por favor.<br>R. No tenga pena. (or, No pasa nada) |

6. Congratulate someone on the birth of a child.

- S. Toutes mes félicitations. J'espère que la mère et l'enfant sont en bonne santé.
- S. Herzlichen Glückwunsch zum freudigen Ereignis.
- S. Felicidades por el neuvo heredero.

7. Console someone who loses a relative.

- S. Mes sincères condoléances. Je partage votre souffrance.
- S. Herzliches Mitleid!
- S. Mi más sentido pésame (por la mierte de tu ____).

8. Indicate to someone that you were joking with them.

- S. Je plaisantais. (Je ne faissis que plaisanter.)
- S. Es war nicht mein Ernst.
- S. Le estoy tomando el pelo.

9. Congratulate someone for just having been married.

- S. Toutes mes félicitations et mes meilleurs voeux du bonheur.
- R. Vous êtes bien gentil (d'être venu).
- S. Alles Gute zur Vermählung!
- S. Felicidades. Que Dios les bendiga en su nueva vida.

10. Thank someone as you leave a party for hospitality extended to you.

- S. Merci infiniment pour votre gracieuse hospitalité.
- R. Je suis très heureux que vous soyez venu.
- S. Vielen Dank fur die Einladung.
- S. Sra., es un placer poder asistir a su fiesta. La fiesta está muy divertida.
- R. Encantada de tenerte. (Es un placer para nosotros que pudiera asistir.)

graphs, traffic signs, comic strips, menus, placards, theater bills, sculptures, caricatures, autographs, slides, movies, newspapers, magazines, books

Tapes and records of popular music, folk songs, classical music, opera, news broadcasts, drama, poetry, interviews, street sounds, conversations, arguments, brawls, jokes, sermons, sirens, air and rail terminal announcements, commentary of museum guides

*To taste*: Bread, cheese, candy, fruit, mustard, mineral water, vegetables, nonalcoholic beverages, condiments, nuts, truffles, olives, regional and holiday specialties

*To smell*: Herbs, perfume, sausage, cheese, soap, flowers, coffee, chocolate, garlic—and all distinctive aromatics

*To touch*: Tickets, travel folders, operational manuals, models, pottery, clothing, toys, *objets d'art,* tools, fabrics, utensils, coins, handcrafted articles, dimensional realia of every description—the range of textures from tapestry to toilet tissue

Whatever is brought into the classroom should be representative of a valid segment of culture, and should be included, directly or tangentially, in the language learning process.

Language students themselves can be actively involved in creating the cultural island. Teacher and students together might develop these or similar suggestions:

1. Make use of the top of classroom walls to display a frieze of continually changing information in the form of lettered placards bearing proverbs, puns, metaphors, similes, regional slurs, slang expressions, riddles, superstitions. Use these as a basis for oral exchange in the classroom.

2. Set up a weathervane and surround it with placards presenting weather sayings, weather small talk, ways to describe every conceivable type of weather.

3. Divide the class into small groups and assign each a city or geographic region for study. Let each group create a mobile with components representative of the outstanding characteristics of the region. Hang the mobiles from the ceiling as a visual focus for the group report.

4. Encourage the artists in the class to contribute to the visual display. *Jewelry designs*—rings, pins, key chains showing variations on favorite motifs (*fleur de lis,* Hapsburg eagle, etc.). *Ceramics*—reproductions of distinctive regional potteries using authentic colors and motifs. *Architecture*—a display of regional prototypes of farmhouses (German: Upper Bavaria, Black Forest, Palatinate, Moselle Valley, Lower Saxony, Hesse/Frankonia). *Other arts*—

depict aspects of the culture using water colors, oils, acrylics, embroidery, collage, *trompe-l'oeil,* sculpture, carving, etc.

5. Share in something living from the target culture. Grow a banana plant, an orange tree, an artichoke, a gum tree, edelweiss, buckwheat. Fill the French classroom window with red and white geraniums as do the citizens of Strasbourg in honor of their regional colors, red and white. Talk about the role the plant plays in the life of the people.

6. Set up a store with tins, packages, and bottles of foreign commodities (empty containers will do). Role-play with foreign currency. Coordinate with advertising slogans and TV commercials. (Send for *Language in the Market Place*, a series of filmed European TV commercials made available for a token fee by the American-Swiss Association, 60 E. 42d Street, New York 10017.)

7. Prepare backdrops for dialogue enactment by projecting colored slides of the foreign country through a hanging sheet. (See Jenks, Frederick L., 1972. "Toward the Creative Teaching of Culture," *American Foreign Language Teacher 2*, 3: 12-14, 42.)

*Activities for the Methods Class.* Discuss the suggestions in this chapter and elicit fresh ideas from the students. Assign the preparation of a different project to each student and work out a rotating basis for changing the displays. As the methods course progresses, the class will be able to see and evaluate many examples of ways to create a cultural island. *Insist that the projects be tied to language learning in a specific way.*

*The Cultural Aside.* The cultural aside is a brief remark dropped into the flow of class activity to illustrate a point of culture. Its entry may be planned, but more often than not it arises spontaneously. The richer the cultural background of the teacher, the more effective his use of this technique. It is the cultural aside—always illuminating, never obtrusive—which acts as the shuttle to inter-weave language and culture. In the following example the curiosity of a beginning German student, studying a photograph in the textbook, provides the entrée for a cultural aside.

> **Student:** Why do they call her Frau Schmidt when she isn't married?
> **Teacher:** What makes you say she isn't married?
> **Student:** Because she doesn't have a wedding ring.
> **Teacher:** Is she wearing any ring at all?
> **Student:** Yes, on her right hand. But no engagement or wedding ring on her left.
> **Teacher:** You're very observant, but sometimes what we see can lead us to the wrong conclusion. In Germany, an engagement ring (usually a plain gold band) is worn on the left hand by both men and women. When they marry,

they simply transfer the ring to the right hand. If Frau Schmidt were a widow, she might wear two bands on her right hand—her own and that of her deceased husband.

*The Slice of Life.* The "slice of life" is an actual segment of the foreign culture brought into the classroom and introduced as the brief focus of learning. It is frequently used as a warm-up device at the beginning of class, but it is equally effective in the slot just before the dismissal bell rings. Its function is to present an authentic "slice of life" that arrests the attention as it instructs. It is accompanied by a few brief comments from the teacher, with time, perhaps, for questions from the students; it must never, however, become an unwieldy addition to the lesson plan.

Examples of the "slice of life" might include two or three "want ads" clipped from a foreign newspaper; a three-minute taped segment of a sportscast from a Canadian or Cuban radio station; a new song popular among French teenagers; or discussion of the latest satirical barb directed at a political figure by a German cabaret group.

*Suggested Reference*

Taylor, James S., 1970. "Direct Classroom Teaching of Cultural Concepts," in (H. Ned Seelye, ed.) *Perspectives for Teachers of Latin American Culture.* Springfield, Ill.: State Department of Public Instruction. pp. 42-50.

*The Culture Capsule.* The concept of the culture capsule was introduced by H. Darrell Taylor and John L. Sorenson (1961). It has since become the basic technique for teaching culture in the American classroom.

The culture capsule is a brief, tightly focused lesson designed to present a point of the target culture which contrasts significantly with the student's own culture. It consists of an informational script written at the language level of the student and accompanied by illustrative material in the form of pictures, diagrams, photos, or dimensional realia.

Taylor and Sorenson (1961) suggested that the script and visuals for any capsule could be devised to fit into a shoebox to be shelved for cooperative use by the language department. A label affixed to each box gives the topic and title of the capsule, the level of proficiency for which it was written, and the machines needed to present any audio-visual aids. During the course of several years, a great many capsules can be developed and filed for departmental use.

A good culture capsule should include reinforcement strategies such as role-playing, discussion, or question and answer techniques to involve the students actively in the new cultural situation. Some form of the inquiry method, whereby students themselves are led to a discovery of the cultural facts, may be used effectively in the capsule approach.

*Suggested References*

Allen, Edward and Rebecca Valette, 1972. In *Modern Language Classroom Techniques, A Handbook.* New York: Harcourt Brace Jovanovich, pp. 265-267.

Miller, J. Dale, 1971. *French Culture Capsules.* Provo (Utah): Brigham Young University.

Taylor, H. Darrell and John L. Sorenson, 1961. "Culture Capsules." *The Modern Language Journal 45*: 350-354. Reprinted in (Seelye, H. Ned, ed.) *A Handbook on Latin America for Teachers.* Springfield, Ill.: Office of Public Instruction. pp. 15-18.

*The Culture Cluster.* A logical extension of the culture capsule is the culture cluster, designed to permit an in-depth exploration of some phase of culture. The cluster is made up of a series of capsules, each self-contained, yet each contributing to the larger configuration. Individual ten-minute capsules presenting different aspects of the central theme are taught daily for three or four days. The series is climaxed by a summarizing activity in the form of a mini-drama or cultural simulation which involves all students in a recapitulation of the cultural material. The culture cluster calls for more sustained organization that the isolated capsule, but it permits investigation in greater detail, allows for re-entry of important concepts, and creates a feeling of suspended excitement as the cluster builds toward the simulation activity.

To illustrate the format of the culture cluster, two outlines developed by students in a class on "Teaching the Cultural Content" at the University of Georgia are presented below.

I.  Culture Cluster Title: *A Day in School in Argentina*

*Level*:     Second or third year of language study

*Time*:     10-15 minutes a day for four days
            Forty-five minutes for the final (fifth day) simulation

*Author*:   Heyde Solano

A.   Cultural attitudes illustrated
     1. Emphasis on order and discipline
     2. Importance of lessons
     3. Importance placed on student's ability to speak before the class
B.   Cultural symbols illustrated
     1. The flag of the country (symbol of patriotism)
     2. The student's uniform: a white coat (symbol of democracy, equality of students)
     3. The school's seal (symbol of pride in institution)
     4. The students' march and song (symbol of pride in age group)

Capsule I.     7:45 a.m.     *Suena le primera campana* (The First Bell Rings)
Capsule II.    8:00 a.m.     *La primera hora de classe* (The First Class Period)

Capsule III.  8:55 a.m.  *El recreo* (Recess Time)
Capsule IV.  12:55 p.m.  *Hasta mañana*! (Until Tomorrow!)
Simulation Activity:  A Day in School


II.  Culture Cluster Title: *Fêtes de Noël en France*

*Level*:   Can be adjusted to meet the demands of any level of French instruction

*Time*:   Each capsule, 15 minutes; audio-motor unit, 10 minutes; simulation activity, 30 minutes

*Author*:   Joseph D. Brewer

A.  Cultural attitudes illustrated
1. Importance of *la famille, le foyer* (shows *un ménage très uni* in both religious and secular events of the Christmas season)
2. Emphasis on order, ceremony, structure
3. *Formules de politesse* (distance-maintaining mechanisms)
4. Importance of *la nourriture, le repas*
5. *L'Amitié*

B.  Cultural symbols illustrated
1. *Le reveillon* (symbol of the unified family)
2. *Le repas du Jour de l'An* (symbol of *le plaisir de table*)
3. *La Médaille de voeux* (symbol of *l'amitié, les souhaits, l'inconnu de l'année nouvelle*)
4. *Le gui* (symbol of immortality)
5. *La carte de visite* (symbol of *la politesse*)

Capsule I;   *La Veille de Nöel*
Capsule II:   *Le Jour de l'An*
Capsule III:   *L'Epiphanie*
Audio-Motor Unit:  *La Galette des Rois*
Simulation:   *La Galette des Rois*


During the course of the cluster, students become actively involved in culture. In the foregoing example, for instance, students not only learn the customs, but how to participate in them as well; they sing the songs, offer the toasts, give the greetings, make the New Year's Resolutions, present the *carte de visite,* and search for the bean in the cake. The final simulation—a dramatization of the Feast of the Kings—enables them to manipulate the language while performing the social rituals. The previous capsules have taught more than the surface manifestations of a holiday ritual. Students have also gained an understanding of the underlying attitudes and assumptions which figure in the French holiday observances.

*Suggested Reference*

Meade, Betsy and Genelle Morain, 1973. "The Culture Cluster." *Foreign Language Annals* (March), pp. 331-338.

## Programmed culture assimilator

An excellent device for presenting cultural information on an individualized basis is the programmed culture assimilator. Designed as a self-contained learning packet, the assimilator usually takes the form of several typed sheets stapled together. The first page presents in a concise narrative a situation giving rise to misunderstanding between representatives of two cultures. The expository paragraph is followed by a choice of four or five answers, each seemingly a plausible explanation for the misunderstanding. The student reads the paragraph and decides which of the answers best accounts for the cross-cultural friction. He then turns to the page corresponding to the answer chosen and sees if his choice is correct. If it is, that page presents a brief explanation of the cultural factors underlying the situation. If it is not correct, the page responds to the reasoning behind the incorrect choice and requests that the student make another selection. The student works through the programmed packet until he has mastered the cultural point in question.

The advantages of the assimilator packets are obvious. They can be grouped as horizontal learning packets to illustrate a major cultural theme (five packets which show varying aspects of *individualisme* in French culture, for instance). Students granted free access to the packets can work at their own speed whenever time permits, absorbing a great deal of information independent of text and teacher. Once familiar with the format, students can write their own programmed packets for use by their classmates. Students can also take a point of culture learned from an assimilator packet and turn it into a mini-drama or culture capsule of their own devising.

In the following example of a programmed culture assimilator, the format has been altered for inclusion in this text. In the original packet, each alternative response is given on a separate page.

### "The End of the Date"

*Directions*: Read the following story of an event which could happen to you if you went to Spain. Then select one of the alternatives that explains what Susan should have done or must do. Turn to the page number of that alternative to see if you have chosen correctly. If you make the wrong choice, select another alternative until you find the correct answer.

*Situation*: Susan, a college girl from the United States, is visiting a friend in Valencia, Spain. Tonight she has gone out on her first date with Rafael, a young Spaniard. Rafael picked her up after supper at 10:00 p.m., took her to the movies, and they have walked home. It is 1:00 a.m.

When they arrive at the door of the *piso,* or apartment building, they find that the door is locked. A feeling of fear runs like a chill down Susan's spine as she remembers that she does not have a key that will open the door. She casts a desperate look at Rafael, who is smiling and unconcerned. What does he expect Susan to know about Spanish customs?

*Alternatives*
1. A young lady in Spain knows exactly what time she will come home and tells the lady (or mother) of the house so that she will be waiting to let her in.

2. If Susan knocks loudly on the door, the *portero* (the person who lives in the downstairs apartment) will let her in.

3. Susan has only to clap her hands twice, very loudly, and an old man will come from somewhere nearby—down the street—to let her in.

4. Susan and Rafael will have to go to the nearest phone, probably in a bar, and call someone in the *piso* to come down and open the door.

*Answers*

*Alternative 1*: As compared to the United States, Spanish people socialize at much later hours than we do. A date might end at 1:00 a.m. or later. Susan would not have known exactly what time she would return. Besides, the lady (or mother) of the house probably has been asleep for hours, unless she too is out with friends. Look for another answer.

*Alternative 2*: Although the *portero* has the key to the outside door, he (or she) is probably asleep and it would not be wise to wake him. The *portero* is in charge of handing out the mail to tenants, of keeping the lobby of his apartment building clean, of opening the outside door in the morning and locking it at about 11:00 p.m. at night. But he does not render the extra service of unlocking the door for everyone who comes in after 11:00 p.m.

*Alternative 3: Correct!* The old man who lives in the neighborhood makes his living from the tips he earns by unlocking the doors of the apartment buildings during late hours. He is called the *sereno.* Many years ago it was his duty to act as a sort of night watchman who walked through the streets and called out the hours as well as the weather conditions. He would say, for example, *"Las tres y despejado."* Today he can be summoned to come and unlock the door of your *piso* if you clap your hands loudly, twice. When he hears your clap he will shout, *"Va-a-a."* You are expected to give him a small tip for his services. Read the other alternatives for more facts you should know.

*Alternative 4*: It is true that there would probably be a bar close by that would still be open, but there is a better alternative. Keep looking.

(Author: Lyla J. Bruhl, student, Department of Language Education, University of Georgia, 1972).

*The Mini-Drama.* The psycho-drama and the socio-drama have been used in other fields as both therapeutic and teaching devices. Because of the close link between language and drama in communication, foreign language teachers have used their own forms of lingua-drama to speed the learning process. The dialogue, a highly structured form of role-playing, was a popular audio-lingual device. Now the term mini-drama has come into use to describe a specialized technique, a brief dramatic script built on a point of disparity between two cultures.

Students, assuming the roles of both native speakers and of visitors in the foreign land, portray scenes of cultural misunderstanding which lead to confusion or hostility. The script brings the actors to a moment of peak frustration and then stops. A discussion follows in which the class tries to analyze the problem. Students gain new insights from this period of exploration and cultural probing. As their knowledge of the foreign culture deepens, so does their perceptiveness of differences in cultural assumptions. By thus placing students in roles where they identify actively with others, the mini-drama helps to develop cross-cultural sensitivity.

The technique is illustrated by the following script written by Seid Ziahosseiny, Language Education doctoral student at the University of Georgia, 1972.

Mini Drama: "You Can't Tell About These Foreigners"

*Characters*: Keith and Michelle, an American couple, on one side of the stage; Seid and Fatima, a Persian couple, on the other side of the stage.

*Setting*: A Persian couple, living temporarily in the United States, have moved into the apartment next door to an American couple. They have made a few tentative efforts to get acquainted. Keith, the American, goes to work and Seid, the Persian, goes to school. They meet about 8:00 in the morning in the parking lot located in the basement of the building. The following scenes show what happens when they return to their apartments in the evening.

**American Couple**

**Keith**: Hi, honey.
**Michelle**: Hi. (They kiss)
**Keith**: What's new?
**Michelle**: Not much. I visited that Persian girl, Fatima, today. She's nice. I think we should get together. I'd like to learn more about the Arabs.
**Keith**: Well, I think they're nuts.
**Michelle**: What do you mean?
**Keith**: They're dumb—stupid. That man upset my stomach this morning.
**Michelle**: Well, calm down. They're not all that important. Would you like something to drink before dinner?

**Keith:** Yes, let's try that foreign wine they gave us the other day. On second thought, forget it. I can't stand anything Persian now. Give me a beer.

**Michelle:** All right, here you are. Now, what happened? I'm dying of curiosity.

**Keith:** Well, this morning, when I was getting into my car to go to work, I saw Seid across the lot. I waved goodby to him. He left his car and hurried toward me. I thought he had something to tell me, but no, he just stood there staring at me. I didn't know what to do. To be honest, I was a little scared. You know—early in the morning—the parking lot—no one around. I just looked at him and smiled. He finally went back to his car. I was five minutes late to work.

**Michelle:** Well, I don't know. Maybe there's something wrong with him. You can't tell about these foreigners.

### Persian Couple

**Seid:** Hi.

**Fatima:** Hi, how was school today?

**Seid:** Fine. How was your day?

**Fatima:** Not bad. Michelle came to visit me. She's so nice.

**Seid:** I think she's nice too. But her husband is a nut.

**Fatima:** Why do you say that?

**Seid:** Oh, I don't know. This morning when I was getting into my car, I saw him smiling as usual. I hate those smiling faces. I can't read them when they smile.

**Fatima:** Isn't it better than frowning?

**Seid:** Yes, but their smile is different. You don't know what is going on in their minds when they smile. Anyway, he called me to go to him.

**Fatima:** I didn't think he could pronounce your name.

**Seid:** Oh, he didn't even bother to call my name. He beckoned me like this (*waves hand*). I thought there was something wrong with his car, so I went over. But he just sat there smiling at me.

**Fatima:** What was wrong with his car?

**Seid:** I never found out. He didn't talk to me. Just kept on smiling. I think he is crazy.

**Fatima:** So what did you do?

**Seid:** I went back to my car and drove to school. He was still there when I drove away.

**Fatima:** I don't know. Maybe there's something wrong with him. I guess we'll never understand these people.

*Class Discussion*

A.  Major cultural points
    1. The American signal for waving goodby means *come here* in Persian culture.
    2. Persians normally try to look solemn during social contacts. Americans smile. In Persia an ever-smiling man is considered insane. An ever-smiling woman is thought to have loose moral standards.

B.  Other cultural points
    1. The Americans assumed that the Persians were Arabs. (Americans lack knowledge about other peoples, especially non-Europeans).
    2. An American man kisses his wife when he returns home. He even kisses her in front of others. Persians do not do this.
    3. Persians give presents to new acquaintances as a sign of respect and friendship; in this case, a bottle of Persian wine.
    4. Americans often have a drink before dinner.
    5. Americans are suspicious, even fearful, of many foreigners.
    6. Americans are uncomfortable pronouncing difficult foreign names. They tend to substitute abbreviated forms or nicknames.

*Suggested References*

Behmer, Daniel E., 1972. "Cultural Mini-Skits Evaluated," *American Foreign Language Teacher II,* 3: 37, 43, 48.

Gorden, Raymond L. *Cross-Cultural Encounter in a Latin American Bank.* A mini-drama produced by Antioch College in cooperation with the Great Lakes Colleges Association.

Snyder, Barbara, 1975. *Encuentros Culturales.* Skokie, Ill.: National Textbook Co.

*The Audio-Motor Unit.* The audio-motor unit, originally developed as a technique for strengthening listening comprehension skills, has proved to be an effective way to impart cultural information.

In the audio-motor unit, the teacher acts out the appropriate responses to a series of taped commands, making use of facial expression, pantomime and gesture to illustrate meaning. Students listen to the tape and watch the actions of the teacher, striving to associate sound with meaning. Then the tape is replayed as the students themselves accompany the teacher in responding to the commands. Through involvement of both audio and motor senses, the student soon absorbs the meaning of the commands and the socio-cultural context as well.

The audio-motor unit is an efficient way to teach points of culture involving movement and emotion. Examples might include making a phone call from a public telephone, boarding a bus, getting a haircut, dining in a restaurant, engaging in an argument, checking a book out of the library, choosing from among the many pastries in a shop, trying on shoes in a store, searching for a lost article, fixing a flat tire, participating in a dance, visiting a doctor, or observing a special celebration. The possibilities for interweaving vocabulary, action, and culture with this technique are endless.

*Suggested References*

Kalivoda, Theodore B., Genelle Morain, and Robert J. Elkins, 1971. "The Audio-Motor Unit: A Listening Comprehension Strategy that Works." *Foreign Language Annals 5:* 392-400.

———, 1972. "Teaching Culture Through the Audio-Motor Unit." *Foreign Language Annals 6:* 61-67.

## Activities for the Methods Class

### Writing Materials

Divide the class into teams and assign each group the responsibility of writing an original culture capsule, culture cluster, mini-drama, programmed culture assimilator packet, or aduio-motor unit. Allow time for the presentation of each type of activity during the course. Request that each team make enough copies of their script so that every member of the class may have one for his teaching file. If videotape equipment is available, tape the presentation for future use.

*Teaching Songs.* The language teacher with a repertoire of foreign songs is in an enviable position. He can use songs linguistically to build vocabulary and reinforce correct use of structure. He can use songs culturally to give his students insights into history and society. The student who sings is participating actively in an authentic segment of living culture.

If the methods course is competency based, one of the skills to be demonstrated might be: "The student will know the words and melody of 10 folk songs and five popular songs and be able to teach them effectively."

The following procedural outline could be used by methods students in teaching a song:

1.  Introduce the song, placing it in its historical or social context. (La cucaracha: Aquí tienen Uds. una canción que cantaban durante la revolución mejicana y que todavía es muy popular.)

2.  Sing the song, or play it on a tape or record.

3.  Make sure the students understand the meaning of the words. Teach vocabulary and explain obscure references. Use visuals, realia, and pantomime as time permits.

4.  Teach pronunciation. Model line by line with repetition by the students. Say the words in the rhythm of the music.

5.  Teach the melody. Set the words to the music line-by-line with repetition by the students.

6.  Lead the class in a spirited rendition of at least one verse of the song. Try to return to the song before the close of the class period. Plan to re-enter it the next day.

7.  When the class has mastered the song, make a tape recording and use that version to teach the song to other classes.

### Suggested References

Juaire, O.F.M., Dennis, 1970. "The Use of Folksongs to Develop Insight into Latin American Culture," in (H. Ned Seelye, ed.) *Perspectives for Teachers of Latin American Culture.* Springfield, Ill.: State Department of Public Instruction. pp. 62-69.

Muñoz, Olivia, 1969. *Songs in the Foreign Language Classroom*. MLA/ERIC Focus Report 12. New York: Modern Language Association Materials Center.

Whiteside, Dale, 1971. "French Music Past and Present: Mini-Lessons in Culture," in (Charles Jay and Pat Castle, eds.) *French Language Education: The Teaching of Culture in the Classroom*. Springfield, Ill.: State Department of Public Instruction.

*Activity for the Methods Class.* Have the songs to be learned by the methods students available on tapes, records, or song sheets. Assign each student one or more songs to be taught in five-minute sessions on different days throughout the course. By the end of the course, all students will know all the songs and each will have had the experience of teaching one. Students can see for themselves how a five-minute break from class routine can refresh and motivate, and how a shared repertoire of songs authentic to the culture can build *esprit de corps* within a group.

## Acquiring cultural information

Knowledge about individual cultures is increasing daily. Techniques for analyzing and teaching culture are being constantly improved. The methods student must be encouraged to follow a career-long quest for cultural information. It is fitting that this chapter conclude with the following alternatives:

1. *Travel in the foreign country.* A teacher with an understanding of the role culture plays in language learning will no longer be content with buying postcards at the Louvre. He will collect realia for the "culture island," make tapes for classroom listening, talk to people of varying cultural backgrounds, and gather anecdotal records which illustrate cultural themes and assumptions.

2. *Community resources.* Native speakers in the community can be a rich source of cultural information. They may be invited into the classroom, or the students may go directly into the language speaking section of the city. The teacher must prepare his students to conduct interviews without antagonizing. This requires a sensitivity to differences in cultural attitudes and assumptions.

3. *Mass media.* Keeping abreast of current developments in the target culture requires disciplined reading of foreign language newspapers and magazines, viewing of foreign films, and listening to foreign language news broadcasts when available.

4. *In-service education.* Workshops and seminars in the area of culture are offered by State Departments of Education and by professional organizations at the state and national level. Universities are developing more courses that focus on cross-cultural understanding and on techniques for analyzing and teaching culture.

5. *Professional reading.* The most accessible sources of information are books and articles in the area of culture. Each year the May issue of *Foreign Language Annals* presents an extensive bibliography with a section devoted to culture. Teachers should also check the publications of such related disciplines as sociology, anthropology, linguistics and psychology for research and development applicable to teaching culture in the foreign language.

Other suggested references given at the end of this book include books and articles that deal with related areas of culture.

## Activities for the methods class

*Developing an Information File.* Ask the students to start a card file, developing their own system for classifying cultural information. Call on them periodically to share references which they consider especially valuable. Encourage them to maintain this file when they become classroom teachers of language and culture.

The day when a foreign language curriculum is defined as containing only four communication skills and culture may well be nearing its end. More and more, a purely cognitive approach to language learning is proving inadequate for meeting the needs of today's students. In an age of instant communication and rapid social change, learners need to relate events in the outside world to their own inner needs. While cognitive training in knowledge and skills may help students comprehend their environment, this training is not always sufficient to help them cope with it. Though students may be equipped with skills to deal with problems, they may not necessarily know which of several possible courses of action to take. That is, students may know how to express a variety of thoughts but are unclear in their own minds as to precisely what they want to say or write. Further, though they may wish to communicate with a speaker of a foreign language in a meaningful way, they may lack the ability to form and sustain human relationships even with speakers of their native tongue. Thus, the foreign language curriculum of the future must comprise more than listening, speaking, reading, writing, and culture. It should prepare students to deal with their own values and feelings; it should enable them to relate meaningfully to themselves as well as to others. The curriculum of the future should encompass an affective dimension.

# 4

# Training Teachers for the Affective Dimension of the Curriculum

47                              *RENÉE S. DISICK*

What is this affective dimension? Is affective education a justifiable part of the foreign language curriculum? If so, how might methods instructors prepare their students to incorporate appropriate training into the curriculum they will teach? What are some problems and limitations of affective education in the foreign language classroom? This chapter will attempt to offer answers to these questions.

## WHAT DOES AFFECTIVE EDUCATION MEAN?

Affective education is a broad term that encompasses two movements that began independently, but are increasingly used together in the classroom: values clarification and human dynamics.

The values clarification movement became influential in the middle 1960s with the publication of *Values and Teaching* by Raths, Harmin and Simon (1966). The authors stated that many students underachieve in school not through lack of cognitive skills, but rather because of confusion in their values. Faced with a multiplicity of diverse and often conflicting role models, authority figures, and life styles, these students are unable to determine clearly to themselves what it is they most prize and what their goals in life should be. As society becomes more complex, the institutions traditionally devoted to the transmission of constant, unchanging values—home, school and church—compete less successfully with peer-group pressures and the alternatives graphically depicted by television and other media. As a result of values confusion, students may view schoolwork as meaningless or purposeless and may react either with apathy or, at the other extreme, with rebellion.

To meet the needs of the ever-growing numbers of students, the values clarification movement offers training in how to choose values intelligently. Rather than attempt to transmit specific values in and of themselves, the movement stresses the importance of the *process* used to select one's lifelong values. Briefly, this process consists of seven steps, some or all of which are present when values are determined consciously and systematically:

*Prizing* one's beliefs and behaviors
1. Prizing and cherishing
2. Publicly affirming, when appropriate
*Choosing* one's beliefs and behaviors
3. Choosing from alternatives
4. Choosing after consideration of consequences
5. Choosing freely
*Acting* on one's beliefs
6. Acting
7. Acting with a pattern, consistency and repetition

Training in values clarification offers exercises—often in small discussion groups—that enable students to determine what values they hold and to practice the steps of the valuing process.

A second part of the affective curriculum encompasses training in "human dynamics." This fairly broad term generally includes the development of self-awareness and self-acceptance, sensitivity toward others, ability to trust and share, and creation of a positive self-image through discovery of one's strengths. "Human dynamics" training offers practice in techniques of active listening, ways of expressing one's real feelings and responding appropriately to the feelings of others, and healthful uses of fantasy and role play.

A philosophic cornerstone of the human dynamics movement is the Basic Needs Theory of Abraham Maslow (1954) as set forth in *Motivation and Personality*. According to this psychologist human beings are motivated by a hierarchy of basic drives. Once lower level needs for physical comfort and safety are fulfilled, people move onward toward seeking love and belongingness, self-esteem and the esteem of others. Man's fifth and highest need is the actualization of his potential ability. That is, what a person *may* be, he *must* become. A self-actualizing individual strives toward the development of a rich and meaningful life, toward creativity, and toward goodness. Though most schools cannot formally teach students to realize their potential, they can, nevertheless, facilitate self-actualization by encouraging examination and comparison of personal values and beliefs, by stimulating creative thinking and real communication among classmates, and by promoting the development of positive self-images in students.

## WHY INCLUDE AN AFFECTIVE DIMENSION IN THE FOREIGN LANGUAGE CURRICULUM?

There are many reasons to make an affective dimension an integral part of a foreign language curriculum. Discussions of values and feelings can promote understanding and tolerance among students. A class atmosphere that encourages acceptance and appreciation of different beliefs and different personalities can respond to the basic needs of students for belongingness, for self-esteem, and for the esteem of others. Furthermore, affective training can contribute significantly to the development of communicative competence[1] in foreign language learners. Affective topics dealing with areas that students are eager to discuss—such as attitudes, preferences, values, dreams, and so on—serve to stimulate more spontaneous communication in the foreign language that goes beyond the mechanistic approach of pattern practices and conventional questions limited to concrete factual areas. Another justification for an affective element in the curriculum is its potentially strong motivational force. Affective exercises are inherently interesting. Students who enjoy opportunities to discuss personally meaningful ideas in a foreign language may become more willing to learn that language. The fluency developed through oral discussions can offer students feelings of success and accomplishment that tend to enhance one's self-image and promote continued learning. Finally, students who have a clearly developed set of values, who think positively of themselves, and who know how to communicate effectively with others are more likely to be receptive to members of the foreign culture and to integrate themselves more easily into it. Similarly, these traits are highly valuable to future teachers of foreign languages.

## HOW CAN FUTURE FOREIGN LANGUAGE
## TEACHERS BE PREPARED TO OFFER AFFECTIVE TRAINING?

Once the foreign language methods teacher has understood the affective dimension of the curriculum and why it is important, he may wish to consider ways of training future teachers in this area. Since this is a relatively new field and personal experience with affective exercises is more the exception than the rule, the instructor would do well to take some preliminary steps to prepare himself for classroom demonstrations of affective activities. A good starting point is reading a wide selection of the professional literature on the topic—both in the field of foreign language as well as in psychology and general education. The bibliography for this chapter at the end of the book is recommended as a source of relevant material. Many instructors will find such preparation sufficient for lecturing on the topic and, perhaps, leading several exercises with student participants. Other instructors, though, will feel more comfortable after having themselves taken part in professionally led training groups. If possible, then, one should try to attend a workshop in values clarification and human dynamics. A brief list of some of these workshops is given at the end of this chapter. Alternatively, a guest lecturer experienced in leading affective exercises may be invited to the methods course to model some successful techniques.

For the methods instructor who chooses to train himself in affective education, certain of the recommended sources in the bibliography will prove immediately helpful. Disick and Barbanel (1974) provide a comprehensive overview of the affective education movement as well as its practical implications in foreign language classrooms. Useful descriptions of language programs with well developed affective dimensions may be found in Born (1974), Christensen (1975), Love and Honig (1973), and Wilson and Wattenmaker (1973b). Practical affective exercises for teachers in any subject area are offered in Harmin, Kirschenbaum, and Simon (1973), Hawley (1975), Hawley and Hawley (1975), Hawley, Simon, and Britton (1973), Hebeisen (1973), Raths, Harmin, and Simon (1966), and Simon, Howe, and Kirschenbaum (1972). Exercises designed specifically for use in foreign language classrooms are provided by Christensen (1975), Gabriel (1973), Morel (1974), Stoller and Lock (1974), Wilson and Wattenmaker (1973a) and the articles by Wolfe (1973) and Wolfe and Howe (1973), and Wolfe, Howe, and Keating (1973).

## HOW MAY AFFECTIVE
## EXERCISES BE USED IN THE METHODS CLASS?

In order to acquaint the methods teacher with some of the techniques frequently used in affective training sessions, a selection of exercises adapted from the material cited above is presented on the following pages. The instructor should feel free to attempt with his methods class those that seem most appropriate and should modify the exercises, if necessary, to suit the particular group of students in his class. He is encouraged to substitute issues of local or current interest for those listed here. Affective training may be incorporated into the methods course in different ways. One or more class hours devoted to lectures and demonstrations may constitute a unit of work in the course. Alternatively, affective exercises lasting from five minutes to an hour may be practiced throughout the duration of the quarter or semester. An advantage of this approach is that as levels of mutual trust between the teacher and his students and among students continue to grow, the sessions become more interesting and more meaningful to the participants. The freer, more open student-teacher relationship that may develop can constitute a sound basis for future professional interchanges, such as student teaching or interning.

A few ground rules should be established so that the experience provides growth for the participants and so that no one feels embarrassed by being compelled to talk about matters he considers personal and private. Students should understand that they may pass any time they do not care to express themselves on any topic. Alternatively, they may make up humorous responses that are not necessarily true. The teacher should explain that he will pose no question that he himself would be unwilling to answer. The class atmosphere should be positive, accepting and noncritical; in no way should student responses be graded or evaluated. In order to avoid overly psychoanalytical sessions that are inappropriate in a methods course, the discussion should be limited to the "Here and Now"—the feelings and experiences shared by students when they are together in class.

## WHAT ARE SOME EXAMPLES OF AFFECTIVE EXERCISES?

Although the affective exercises presented here are intended for use with prospective teachers, their content can be adapted to suit the language level, maturity, and interests of language learners in college, high school, junior high or elementary school.

### Values voting

The teacher presents orally a series of five to ten values statements and asks students to vote either for or against each. After each vote, volunteers express the reasons for their choices. This exercise serves to make students aware of what their values are and which people agree and disagree with them. It provides opportunities to affirm one's beliefs publicly and exposes students to a variety of opinions against which they may evaluate the ideas they hold. Some values statements might be:

> *How many of you. . .*
> . . .prefer full-class instruction to individualized instruction?

. . .intend to be stricter with your students than your teachers were with you?

. . .are optimistic about the future of foreign language instruction in this country?

. . .are satisfied with the way this college/university is run?

. . .are enjoying this exercise?

This exercise may take from ten to twenty minutes of class time. If it proves successful, students may write lists of questions to be used during future sessions. The linguistic level is appropriate for intermediate or advanced students.

## Rank order

Students see lists of three or more choices and rank them in order of preference. Then, they discuss their reasons for their choices.

*Examples:*

The most important traits for an effective teacher are:

_____ tolerance _____ cheerfulness _____ organization _____ intelligence _____ sincerity

The most important qualities in a spouse are:

_____ generosity _____ faithfulness _____ ambition _____ sense of humor _____ understanding

After each discussion, students may wish to revise their rankings as a result of having listened to different points of view. This exercise offers students practice in choosing values after examining several alternatives. Depending on the length of discussion and number of items the exercise may last from ten to thirty minutes. This exercise is suited to intermediate or advanced students.

## Forced choice

Class furniture is arranged so that students may pass easily from one side of the room to the other. The teacher reads a list of either/or choices and students walk to the side designated for his opinion. Once there he chooses a partner and they discuss their ideas for one or two minutes. When the teacher calls "time," participants return to the center of the room and regroup for the next choice. Some possible forced choices:

Are you. . .

. . .more like a rose or a daisy?

. . .more like patent leather or suede?

. . .more like summer or winter?

. . .more yes or no?

. . .like a clothesline or a kite string?

This is a good exercise for breaking the ice at the beginning of an intermediate or advanced course. It serves to stimulate thinking about one's self-concept and values and can last approximately fifteen minutes.

## Values continuum

On the blackboard or on dittoed handouts the teacher draws a line to represent the continuum of opinion between opposing values. Students mark with a cross or with their initials the point on the line that seems to represent their beliefs. Students may arrange themselves physically according to their choices and express their feelings on the topic. For example:

What percentage of your waking hours do you enjoy spending alone?
0% _____ 100%
How patriotic are you?
    Apathetic                                              Flag-waving
    Al          _____- Flora
How neat are you?
    Super-neat                                           Slovenly
    Sarah        _____ Sol
What are your reading habits?
    Nothing that's                                   Bookworm
    not assigned    _____ Betsy

In addition to helping students and teacher become acquainted, this exercise demonstrates that a variety of values exist in class and no one set of values is right for each individual. It encourages tolerance and understanding of other people. This same technique may be employed with issues such as race, religion, politics, and sex. About fifteen minutes can be allowed, and the exercise may be modified for use with beginning students.

## Exercises in life examination

In an intermediate or advanced class the teacher distributes to students an outline drawing of a coat of arms divided into a half-dozen numbered sectors. Below the drawing are six questions. Students respond by drawing symbols of their answers in the spaces on the coat of arms corresponding to the number of each question. After completing their answers (out of class, preferably) students explain their responses in small groups of four to six. Questions suitable for this exercise include:

What do you consider your greatest personal achievement to date?

What do you consider your greatest personal failure to date?

What is one thing you do to make other people happy?

What one thing can others do to make you happy?

If you had one year to live, how would you spend it?

What three things would you most like to have said about you if you died today? (Words may be used instead of drawings)

This exercise encourages intermediate or advanced students to think about what they are doing with their lives and whether they are actively directing them in accordance with their values. Students should feel free to leave blanks if they choose not to answer certain questions. They are also not compelled to explain their drawing if they do not want to. An alternative to small group discussion is a gallery walk along a wall where the coats of arms are posted and students talk about their work. The time allowed may be from twenty to forty minutes.

### Interview techniques

Students volunteer to come to the front of the room to be interviewed by the rest of the class. The person is free to pass on any question he wishes and to pose the same question to the person who asked it after his turn is ended. Each interview can last up to five minutes and may be terminated when the teacher or student says, "Thank you for the interview." Some appropriate questions are:

What do you plan to do this coming vacation?

What are some of your hobbies?

What are your favorite TV shows?

What books have most influenced your life?

What person do you most admire?

What are some things you really believe in?

As the trust level in the class grows, the questions in subsequent sessions may relate to more sensitive issues, such as:

What is your position on marijuana?

Whom will you support in the next election?

Do you have friends of other races and religions?

How do you feel about homosexuality?

Do you practice your religion?

Have you ever cheated in school?

If you were the teacher of this class, what would you do differently?

In addition to helping students become better acquainted, the interview promotes self-examination and affirmation of one's values publicly. Initially, the teacher may wish to distribute in advance a list of interview questions; these may be supplanted, however, by material composed by class members. The first time that this exercise is presented the teacher may play the role of interviewee in order to show students that the exercise is not threatening. Questions may be selected to suit the linguistic competence of beginning students.

## Incomplete sentences

Incomplete sentences can be used when as little as ten minutes of class time are available. Students hear a sentence stem and supply their own completions.

*Examples*:
What I most enjoy doing is. . .
What I least enjoy doing is. . .
I'm happy that. . .
I'm annoyed/unhappy that. . .
If I could do whatever I wanted. . .
I am. . . (a noun or adjective completion)

Another use for incomplete sentences is summarizing the results of other affective exercises at their conclusion.

Some stems can be:
I realized that. . .
I learned that. . .
I feel that. . .

This type of exercise is particularly suited to beginning language learners since its controlled structure makes it resemble a pattern drill—but an enjoyable one, since students contribute their own ideas and feelings to it.

## Communication circles

In groups of no more than fifteen, intermediate or advanced students share their thoughts, about one or more discussion topics such as the following:

What have you done that makes you feel good?

Is there a person you dislike intensely? What makes you feel that way about him or her?

Is there something that you have said or done that you have regretted?

What has been a difficult decision for you?

What would you like to change about yourself, your best friend, or a member of your family?

A variation on this exercise calls for group members to paraphrase or "reflect" the answers of each individual, beginning with, "You. . ." This activity promotes freer self-expression and listening skills. The opportunity to share meaningful ideas in a positive and receptive atmosphere builds feelings of self-worth and shows students that their experiences are not necessarily unique and that others have gone through similar circumstances. The Human Development Program adapted for language teaching by Wilson and Wattenmaker (1973a) makes extensive use of this technique.

### Fantasy exercises

On a blank sheet of paper students list the ten people they see most often—friends, teachers, and family members. Next, they circle up to three people with whom they are having a disagreement or conflict or to whom they need to say something they have withheld.

On the reverse side of the paper, students make three columns and label them, "I resent that you. . . ," "I demand that you. . . ," and "I appreciate that you. . ." Imagining that they are talking to one of the people circled, students write in the appropriate space what they resent in the person's actions, what they want him to do to rectify the situation, and indicate their understanding of his point of view. Volunteers may share their responses with other members of the class. This exercise for intermediate or advanced students will proceed effectively if the teacher offers his own responses as examples before asking students to write theirs.

In another fantasy exercise students close their eyes, and the teacher directs them to imagine themselves in the place they would most like to be, doing what they most want to, and talking to the people they most want to see. Several minutes are allowed for students to do this. After being told to return to the classroom and to open their eyes when ready, students may share their fantasies if they wish, either in pairs or before the entire class.

An important psychological basis of fantasy exercises is the Gestalt Theory of Frederick Perls (1971) who emphasizes the individual's need for completeness or wholeness. According to Perls any imbalance or lack of resolution of an important matter prevents a human being from functioning effectively as an integrated organism. Though conflicts may not always be resolved in daily life, an individual may achieve his necessary balance through imagination and fantasy. Increasingly structured meditation sessions and active mind control are gaining acceptance. They are considered therapeutic because they help people relax and escape from the pressures of daily reality. What cannot always be achieved in actual experience may be accomplished through fantasy—with similarly satisfying and even beneficial effects on the individual. A corollary of Perls' view of human nature is that education should be aimed at the *whole* individual, not at isolated parts. It should encompass both the thinking *and* feeling aspects of each human being.

Fantasy exercises are appropriate for intermediate or advanced students but may work best in groups where the level of trust is high and where participants are intelligent and possess lively imaginations. They are nevertheless useful in average groups as a stimulus toward greater self-expression and creative thinking. An exercise may be completed in about a quarter of an hour.

## WHAT ARE SOME FOLLOW-UP
## ACTIVITIES TO THE AFFECTIVE EXERCISES?

Once the methods instructor has lead several different types of affective exercises in class—either the ones presented here or those listed in the recommended sources—there are many follow-up activities that can prove useful to future teachers. First of all, it is a good idea to ask for students' reactions at the end of each of the exercises. This feedback can provide the instructor with information necessary to modify or improve the techniques used in class. This may be accomplished most naturally through openended, incomplete sentences (as mentioned above) or by written evaluations handed in to the teacher.

If the reactions are generally positive, students may be assigned to work in this area, perhaps as one of the choices for a course project or instead of a written paper. After reading widely in the sources recommended by the teacher, students may write their own affective exercises. In their work, it is essential that they state the age-level and language-level for which they think it appropriate and its format: Full class, small groups (of how many?) or pairs. They should also show an awareness of the level of mutual trust they believe is necessary by indicating whether the exercise is suitable for the beginning, middle, or end of the course or whether it may be appropriate at all times. Each activity should include a specific affective purpose and the approximate amount of time required. It is especially important that students devise simple exercises appropriate at the beginning levels of language since limited structure and vocabulary at this stage of learning make such actvities difficult to find; yet, high attrition rates prevalent after the early language courses suggest an urgent need for affective exercises in these classes.

Once the instructor has checked and approved the written material, students should have the opportunity to explain their exercises and lead the class in them. This may be accomplished in a number of ways. If the methods class is small, it might be most convenient to conduct the exercise with the entire group. Alternatively, part of the class may volunteer to participate while the rest serve as observers. In either case, the student leader should receive positive feedback after the experience and should be encouraged to evaluate his own efforts. This activity also lends itself to the micro-teaching format in which videotaped activities are critiqued by the methods teacher and by students.

Depending on the fluency and linguistic command of the students, the instructor may ask that the exercises be conducted either in English or in the foreign language. In methods classes where students from different languages are together, as is quite common, the exercises may be in English or the class may divide into language groups that the instructor supervises as he moves about the room. In any event, when a foreign language is used, grammar and pronunciation errors *must never* be corrected as this would stifle the free self-expression being encouraged and thus defeat the purpose of the experience which is primarily affective, rather than cognitive.

## WHAT ARE SOME LIMITATIONS AND
## PROBLEMS OF AFFECTIVE TRAINING?

A discussion of affective training would be incomplete without mentioning its pitfalls, limitations, and problems. First, it is unlikely that all methods teachers will accept it. Even among those who believe in the value of this training, not everyone will feel comfortable and successful leading affective exercises. This is right and as it should be. The foreign language profession embraces a wide variety of personalities and people whose methods and techniques vary considerably. This is a strength of the profession. Though affective exercises may be suitable for every methods instructor, they do, nevertheless, represent an alternative to be considered. Some may wish to include affective training in a methods course; others may not. These responses are appropriate to a relatively new movement in the foreign language field, a movement that has not yet been evaluated in a variety of circumstances over a considerable period of time.

Similarly, methods teachers who perform effectively in this area need to realize that the students who experience initial success leading affective exercises will probably constitute a minority of the class. Just as the number of students capable of leading a lively discussion is small, so it is true with values clarification and human dynamics exercises that require not only cognitive skills but affective ones as well. However, students often lack needed discussion skills precisely because they are judged incapable of this activity and therefore are afforded few or no opportunities during their schooling to cultivate these important behaviors. For this reason, it is important that methods teachers afford willing students a supportive environment in which they may grow as human beings and develop the skills and sensitivity needed to lead affective exercises. Though the day is far off when performance in this area will be considered part of the minimal competence required for certification, affective training may nevertheless ultimately prove to be among the most important and valuable experiences that students take with them from the methods course.

Some caveats are in order before students employ affective exercises in their own foreign language classes. They should understand that these activities are appropriate for dealing with the typical concerns of growing youngsters and young adults. In no way are they intended for use as psychotherapy for individuals with specialized or severe emotional problems. Discussions, therefore, should be structured so as to discourage highly personal self-revelations. This may be accomplished by limiting the amount of speaking time allowed each individual and by changing the focus to another member of the group. Should the teacher suspect a psychological disturbance, he may privately recommend that professional help be sought.

Prospective users of these exercises should also be aware that not all communities are receptive to discussions of personal values and feelings. If a teacher senses that parents in his highly conservative community would object vociferously to this type of activity in class, he should not attempt it. Even in more liberal circumstances, he would be well advised to maintain considerable discretion when initiating affective sessions. There is no need, for example, to announce to students that they will explore their innermost values or feelings. Rather, the cognitive aspect of the exercise—perhaps a certain grammar topic, or conversation skill—can be stressed. The exercise may be introduced by telling students they will have a chance to talk in the foreign language about some of the things they believe in or some of the things they feel, since differences and similarities among class members can be very interesting. The teacher should make clear that students need not speak if they feel they have nothing to contribute to a particular topic. A selection of impersonal and unthreatening exercises can render this statement superfluous.

Some prospective teachers may voice concern over the difficulty of finding enough class time for affective exercises and yet complete the designated curriculum for the year. In this situation, the methods instructor might tell his students what provisions he made in his own class to accommodate this unit. He may point out ways in which class time is normally wasted and how it might be used more effectively for these activities. Or, he may suggest how judicious cuts may be made in the curriculum so as to release additional class time for affective discussions. For example, some grammar topics (such as formation of adverbs) might be treated as vocabulary, rather than being accorded the same amount of attention deserved by verbs, pronouns, and syntactical topics. Basically, though, the issue is one of values and goals. If a teacher believes his highest function is to drill vocabulary and grammar, then these activities will predominate. If, however, he feels that his most important role is personalizing the cognitive training offered in textbooks and allowing students to discover themselves and their values while learning a foreign language, then he will invariably find ways of mkaing the time needed to acomplish these higher goals.

## DOES AFFECTIVE EDUCATION WORK?

Perhaps the greatest limitation of affective education in language teaching today is the lack of statistical proof regarding its effectiveness. Though little scientific evidence exists to justify most of the common methods employed in language classes, many practitioners hestitate to adopt a relatively new highly personal approach without reasonable assurance that it will work. Therefore, until controlled experimental data become available, it is important that teachers who employ affective techniques in methods courses as well as in language classes report the results of their experiences, both positive and negative. The relative brevity of the foreign language bibliography for this chapter (at the end of the book) is an indication of the need for considerably more research in this area. For instance, information concerning the impact of affective techniques on maintaining and increasing foreign language enrollments is vital to a meaningful evaluation of this area of the curriculum. To date published reports of practical classroom experiences by Christensen (1975), Morel (1974) and Wilson and Wattenmaker (1973b) indicate that affective exercises substantially increase students' motivation and interest and promote their ability to communicate in the foreign language. These encouraging findings need to be repeated on a wide-scale basis.

In summary, affective education, composed of ideas from the values clarification and human dynamics movements, has been described. Arguments suggesting the necessity for this training in the foreign language methods course have been presented along with a bibliography of recommended sources of general information and specific exercises. Ways of managing affective activities in class as well as proposals for follow-up projects by students should help instructors implement them in their classrooms. It should be recognized, however, that not all instructors or future teachers can be expected to possess the skills and sensitivity required to lead effective discussions. Those intending to use affective exercises need to be aware of the possible abuses and misuses in this area and should take precautions to act with discretion. The affective dimension of foreign language training is a relatively new area that deserves further exploration. Case studies published so far suggest that affective exercses do, indeed, promote foreign language learning, but more research is needed.

Affective education may ultimately turn out to be a fad that passes with the '70s; or, it may become one of the most exciting frontiers of the 1980s. The course the movement will take will be determined to a considerable extent by the responses of methods instructors and the foreign language teachers they prepare.

## SOME WORKSHOPS IN AFFECTIVE EDUCATION

1. Achievement Motivation Program, W. Clement and Jessie V. Stone Foundation, 111 East Wacker Drive, Suite 510, Chicago, Illinois 60601.

2. The Adirondack Mountain Humanistic Education Center, Springfield Road, Upper Jay, New York 12987.

3. Center for Studies of the Person, 1125 Torrey Pines Road, La Jolla, California 92037.

4. Confluent Education Development and Research Center, P.O. Box 30128, Santa Barbara, California 93105.

5. Esalen Institute, Big Sur Hot Springs, Big Sur, California 93920.

6. Human Development Training Institute, 4455 Twain Avenue, Suite H, San Diego, California 92120.

7. National Training Laboratories Institute for Applied Behavioral Science, 1201 16th St. N.W., Washington, D.C. 20036.

8.  Parent Effectiveness Training Courses and Teacher Effectiveness Training Associates, 110 South Euclid Avenue, Pasadena, California 99101.

9.  Real Communication in Foreign Language. Beverly Wattenmaker, 4162 Giles Road, Chagrin Falls, Ohio 44022. Virginia Wilson, P.O. Box 1310, Fairbanks, Alaska 99401.

10. Institute for Reality Therapy, William Glasser, M.D., President, 11633 San Vicente Boulevard, Los Angeles, California 90049.

11. Values Clarification Workshops, Values Associates, Box 43, Amherst, Massachusetts 01002.

## NOTE

[1]See Sandra J. Savignon *Communicative Competence: An Experiment in Foreign-Language Teaching.* Philadelphia: Center for Curriculum Development, 1972.

## UNIT STRUCTURE

In developing a unit on individualization for students in foreign language methods classes, we first need to decide on the format for the course. In a seminar given in Chicago in late 1971, Altman (1972a) suggested a lecture-discussion-observation unit of about eight to ten hours in length within the framework of a regular foreign language methods program. Another approach individualizes that portion of the foreign language methods course which deals with individualized instruction itself. Smith (1972) goes even further and recommends that the entire course be individualized. Whatever the format, some structure for a proposed unit must be established early in the planning stage.

This chapter discusses a number of classroom activities to aid candidate-teachers in acquiring techniques and procedures for individualizing foreign language instruction. The methods instructor may wish to choose several of the sections below for use, as in the Smith proposal, or to devote a special unit of the foreign language methods course to individualization.

---

# 5

# Individualized Instruction and the Foreign Language Methods Course

*ROBERT A. MORREY*

# INTRODUCING INDIVIDUALIZATION

Since individualization of instruction is a rather new concept, we should present candidate-teachers with a general overview of individualized foreign language programs before discussing their respective characteristics. What is the historical background for individualization? On the one hand, many teachers have long felt that they could not satisfy the needs of the fast learners and slow learners in their classes by "teaching to the middle of the class." In addition, high school students are assuming more responsibility for selecting their courses and are avoiding elective classes which do not offer challenging and pleasant learning experiences. Teachers who have successfully individualized programs feel that they are able to offer a good program to students who learn rapidly as well as to those who need more time. In addition, they occasionally can provide alternative activities or materials which allow students to study topics of special interest in greater depth. These two basic factors stimulate student interest and motivation, thereby contributing to a more harmonious learning environment. It seems that this rationale for a change in approach is sound, and that individualization of instruction is, indeed, one possible solution to the problems spawned by "teaching to the middle of the class."

In order to introduce our methods students to the concept of individualization, certain general classroom activities may be helpful. The methods course instructor should require his students to read articles which describe types of individualized programs; those by Altman (1971), Bockman and Gougher (1971-1975), Morrey (1972) and Steiner (1971) might be included. The class activities should include a discussion of the general scope and sequence of individualized programs.

Class discussion might profit from the presence of local teachers engaged in individualized programs or from a series of slides, photographs or videotapes of ongoing courses.

# DEFINING INDIVIDUALIZATION

After this introduction it seems fitting for the methods class to consider some definitions of the topic. In writings of Altman and Politzer (1971) and Logan (1970), individualized instruction has been characterized as a student-centered instructional program in which the student is allowed to move through pre-packaged materials at his own pace. In order to capitalize on the student's internal motivation and unique learning habits, the foreign language classroom teacher allows him to proceed at his own pace by a series of controlled teaching and measurement techniques.

Altman (1972b) lists a number of principles for individualized programs which, he feels, distinguish individualization as a philosophy of education, rather than as an approach or method of teaching. This philosophy embraces the academic, attitudinal and motivational needs of the student as potentially different from each of his classmates. Accordingly, the student's characteristics may determine curricular and instructional priorities. Stated differently, no specific "method" is automatically a necessary component of the philosophy of individualized instruction. Provision for individual differences is not the distinguishing trait of any given method. Any school can provide for individual differences, be it the most modern or the most outmoded physical plant. We must urge candidate-teachers to deal with individual differences whatever the classroom method. To the extent that, at least at certain points in time, the student feels that his own needs are being met by the teacher's presence and activity, his teacher has individualized instruction.

*Classroom* projects for this section on definition should be designed to provide the candidate-teacher with guidelines for developing an individualized program. Methods students might be asked to:

1. assess opinions on the validity of the basic principles stated by Altman and by Altman and Politzer;

2. apply Altman's principles for individualization to the different types of programs described by Logan;

3. formulate the basic structure for an individualized program around a given topic or grammatical point, using Altman's principles; this project might represent an ongoing sequence as methods students mature and become familiar with the textbooks they will one day use.

## PROBLEMS IN INDIVIDUALIZATION

As one expects with any approach to instruction, certain problems become evident in individualized foreign language programs. Steiner (1971) has mentioned some of these; others merit attention as well. At this point in the foreign language methods class presentation, candidate-teachers should be cognizant of these disadvantages as they proceed in their evaluation of alternative programs. The first problem is the *redefinition of the role of the teacher*. In recent articles by Allen (1971), Altman (1971), Steiner (1971) and Valette and Disick (1972), certain major aspects of the teacher's changing role come to light. Unfortunately for the foreign language student and for the candidate-teacher, the teacher's role (as pictured in the above articles) is only a rather one-sided account. All these articles stress the importance of *systems management activities*; this set of activities represents the first major aspect of the teacher's changing role. The systems management aspect, in turn, is composed of the two functions, system design and coordination, and curriculum development. Altman (1971) summarizes current thought on the teacher's role:

> . . .the task of the foreign language teacher in an individualized program is to *manage and facilitate the learning process.* Note that the emphasis in the teacher's role is no longer on teaching, but rather on managing and facilitating what students learn.

From my personal experience as a foreign language teacher and as observer of individualized foreign language programs, I concur that the systems management aspect is crucial to a successfully individualized foreign language program. I believe that certain of these systems management skills can be acquired through readings such as those mentioned above. Other skills can be learned through guided observation of local foreign language programs.

Complementary to the systems management role, the heart of Altman's thinking, I would propose a second, an *instructional role* for the teacher, composed of a diagnostic/prescriptive function and a motivational function. Under the designation "diagnostic/prescriptive," I classify all the activities of the teacher which normally would be described as instruction in a traditional program, that is, presentation of material to one or more students, explanations of grammar concepts, etc. The teacher must be able to analyze errors, to describe the student's learning strategy, to develop a hypothesis about the reasons for errors or mistakes (that is, his diagnosis), test his hypothesis against student performance and, finally, indicate to the student how he can solve the problem (that is, his prescription).

I would suggest that candidate-teachers, and especially those preparing for individualized programs, be required to conduct a number of classroom activities designed to enhance instructional abilities.

1. The candidate-teachers should teach a concept to the foreign language methods class and then obtain feedback on performance; this activity would perhaps best be delayed until after the students have acquired the ability to use techniques for composing lesson plans for individualized units.

2. Candidate-teachers should be provided with samples of students' work and be required to propose diagnoses of difficulties and suggestions for solutions.

3. If possible, candidate-teachers should work with foreign language students, preferably in an individualized program, and determine their successes, their problems and appropriate remedies.

The motivational role of the teacher is perhaps the most neglected aspect of his function, and yet motivation is probably one of the most important domains of the foreign language teacher's classroom situation. Here the ability of a teacher to motivate students is the ability to create a positive learning atmosphere, to relate to students as individuals, to express interest in each person's achievement and to interact in positive favorable ways.

In the course of my observations I have noted that student achievement diminishes (in quantity and quality) when foreign language teachers lack motivating skills. Informed of protest by parents and colleagues, these foreign language teachers introduced types of external pressure; they required the students to complete small increments every day and record their own progress on individual record sheets. Valette and Disick (1972) document this problem and describe how a foreign language teacher had to institute a coercive system, a negative approach to motivation, including a procedure for deducting points from the student's grade whenever the student achieved less than eighty per cent on a test.

Such diminution of student achievement is, I believe, a consequence of at least two factors. First, the students had not been sufficiently made aware of the external procedures and responsibilities characteristic of an individualized system. Second, the teacher had not been able to establish adequate "internal" motivation for student learning. It is understandable that the students may have lacked a certain sense of responsibility to achieve in a low-pressure foreign language class, since students have for many years been trained to do only what their teachers assigned. Consequently, when students enter an individualized foreign language program and are told, in effect, "Here's the material. You can work as fast as you want," the student thinks, "Boy, I don't have to do anything. No homework, tests when (or if) I want them. This is great." But the wise candidate-teacher who tries to abandon overt controls institutes other types of less visible controls. At first, he shows how the program works. He may have students complete certain small assignments with short time limits, with the implicit encouragement to do additional work on their own, such as reading a comic book in a foreign language, looking at a slide-tape program, etc. After a time, the candidate-teacher may begin to relax his controls and give more freedom to those students who demonstrate their ability to utilize resources well.

In the area of motivation, some research results, reported by Gardner and Lambert (1972), Hanzeli and Love (1972) and Teetor (1972), and a great deal of personal observation underline the foreign language teacher's importance in establishing both an appropriate atmosphere for learning and for fostering internal motivation. In other words, there is basis for believing that students can be taught a foreign language, and that they can learn also to like that foreign language.

I strongly believe that candidate-teachers can be taught to utilize techniques for improving the classroom climate and for motivating students. One of the most effective and best documented current methods of improving the foreign language student/teacher relationship is interaction analysis. See, for example, Flanders (1970), Moskowitz (1968; 1970; 1972), and Papalia and Zampogna (1972). Interaction analysis employs an inventory of verbal behavior in the classroom. The primary advantage of this technique accrues from an increased awareness of the relationship between stated goals and observed behavior.

In addition to the observations by Disick (1972), Nelson et al. (1970), and Papalia and Zampogna (1972), which are oriented toward foreign language learning, two areas of educational psychology support the concept of the motivational role. Candidate-teachers should know how to apply basic principles of learning theory and motivation to foster optimum learning experiences.

The candidate-teacher should be encouraged to foster motivation in language classes by acting as a facilitator rather than a policeman. He should be taught to use grading procedures based on criteria other than those dictated by the curve of normal distribution. Further, he should be assisted in learning to write various forms of tests to permit his students to test and retest themselves until an adequate level of mastery is reached. These activities should be practiced in the methods class in a situation (cf., Arendt (1971), Buchanan (1971), and Papalia and Zampogna (1972)) which allows the candidate-teacher a chance to teach small segments to be evaluated by the methods teacher and methods class. If the methods class is fortunate enough to arrange a small class of "students" other than the candidate-teacher's peers, peer teaching can be profitably avoided. Interaction analysis, as explained above, and diagnosis of motivational problems contribute to a further knowledge of the effects of learning conditions on student motivation. Both teacher roles in individualized instruction, viewed here as complementary aspects of teacher behavior, point to the learner-centered classroom as pivotal to improved foreign language instruction.

A second problem deals with the *development of oral proficiency*. Many teachers have felt that individualized instruction, with its seeming premium on self-pacing and self-help, would unduly neglect conversational skills more properly cultivated in group situations. The candidate-teacher should be aware that the laboratory study carrel with its tape-slide programs must be complemented by a program designed for the acquisition and refinement of oral production skills along the lines of the suggestions in recent articles by Logan (1970), Morrey (1972), Rivers (1971 and 1972). Both Arendt (1970) and Ryberg and Hallock (1972) voice their concern that independent study not totally replace the dynamics and communication of a closely knit foreign language class.

Candidate-teachers might not be alert to this second area of major concern due to their relative personal inexperience with individualized programs. They might profitably work in one or more of these projects to focus on the dynamics of large group foreign language study. The foreign language methods class should discuss the readings with thorough attention to theoretical issues and practical guidelines for developing conversational proficiency in individualized programs. Candidate-teachers should be asked to design a short unit based on specific oral skills in conjunction with taped or workbook materials they will use during their student teaching. They should reassess their ongoing lesson plans with particular care that individualized instruction provide ample large group practice in oral proficiency.

A third problem concerns a *desire to individualize too quickly*. The need here is to avoid rapid individualization with inferior or hastily prepared materials and to concentrate instead on a moderate process of individualization spanning an extended period of time. While materials are being developed certain aspects of an individualized program may be immediately integrated into traditional programs: a retest policy which provides for parallel multiple forms of the same test, grades equated with proficiency levels, and "optional" review sessions during the class. These sessions are designed to provide further practice for those students who are having difficulty with a particular concept. Long-range planning is described by

Clark (1971), Dellaccio et al. (1971), and McKim (1972) who propose practical guidelines for the implementation of individualized foreign language programs.

Candidate-teachers need to know about the development of materials for individualized programs. The fact that only a very few are now commercially produced makes this matter a fourth problem for the methods class to deal with. A recent book by Helen Davis Dell (1972) presents excellent documentation and a good bibliography outlining the preparation of instructional objectives and learning guides. Rosenthal (1973) has written succinctly of the learning activity package (LAP), and Kapfer and Swenson (1968) have characterized the UNIPAC. Mueller (1971) sketches a number of practical points for constructing materials, notably programmed materials, and Hocking (1971) discusses the benefits of machine-aided learning. A recent Northeast Conference Report (1969) surveys the design, construction, and use of a large variety of audiovisual aids. Finally, Arendt (1970) and Logan (1970) appraise existing individualized foreign language materials and refer to supplementary materials.

Materials development is an art to which many professionals aspire, so that it seems fitting that candidate-teachers be supplied with a checklist pertinent to single-concept units or to learning packets. The foreign language methods instructor might begin with these:

1. make directions extremely clear with simple language;

2. illustrate and clarify with concrete examples;

3. delineate each topic clearly and reserve extraneous material and exceptions for later units;

4. vary the sense mode and format of each unit;

5. provide cultural material routinely through a variety of traditional and innovative sources.

Candidate-teachers should prepare a range of LAP's or UNIPAC's to accommodate a specific chapter in the text they will use during student teaching. However, candidate-teachers must be aware that a wide range of quality will thus result. Teacher-made materials are neither more nor less sound, by definition, than commercially prepared materials.

Since individualized foreign language instruction involves a basic component of systems management, *classroom organization* presents a fifth problem for candidate-teacher consideration. Physical layout of the classroom relates to instructional activities in the same way that compilation of instructional materials stems from the scope and sequence of foreign language curricula. Pronunciation exercises, grammar presentation, reading selections, listening comprehension segments and cultural topics shape a recognizable whole, yet the systems management concept requires that subsections present achievable and satisfying learning tasks. *Spanish for Communication* (Bull, et al., 1971) and *Individualized*

*Foreign Language Learning: An Organic Process* (Logan, 1973) offer models for the compilation of individualized instructional materials.

The foreign language student's progress through these materials may follow one of two widely accepted patterns. "Routing" serves to direct students through predetermined material at their own pace, notably in the elementary foundation courses. "Contracts" allow the student to choose the material he studies and the pace at which he is to progress (Bockman, 1971). Options such as those which allow partial course credit regardless of course completion are frequently integral parts of individualized foreign language programs. However, administrative complications may force some candidate-teachers to abide by standard grading procedures despite their partially individualized programs (Logan, 1971). Record-keeping (see Braswell, 1972; Clark, 1971; Dell, 1972) should assist the teacher in monitoring individual, incremental progress leading toward the completion of a contract or a unit of work. Students should have access to these records.

## GUIDED OBSERVATIONS

Busse, in her chapter in this volume, refers to the need for knowledgeable observations, where candidate-teachers focus attention on certain aspects of teacher behavior. The previous section on program structure, credits and recordkeeping points to areas where candidate-teachers should observe classroom practice in individualized foreign language programs. The foreign language methods instructor must introduce these major issues in class, and then identify them during guided observations, each of which focuses on only one specific portion of teacher behavior.

## OBSERVATION CHECKLIST

a)    How satisfied do foreign language students appear? What observations support this judgment?

b)    What kind of interaction profile does the teacher present?

c)    Does classroom space contribute to effective individual and group work?

d)    Who wrote the materials and what are their purposes and suitability?

e)    How adequately is teacher behavior devoted to various tasks?

f)    How are records maintained and how is credit achievement filed?

g)    How proficient are the students in the various skills of the target language?

h)    What motivational activities does the teacher employ?

i)    How satisfied does the teacher appear? What observations support this judgment?

The extent to which candidate-teachers can successfully practice teach in an individualized setting enhances their ability to identify (through guided observations) behavior appropriate to individualized foreign language programs. Berwald (1974) has developed an eleven point checklist which supervisors might consult to further orient candidate-teachers; the same checklist serves to evaluate on-the-spot practice teaching.

## CONCLUSION

In this chapter I have presented a number of ideas about the design, organization and conduct of individualized foreign language programs to be discussed in the methods course. The problem areas I have characterized are those that may cause difficulties for foreign language teachers and candidate-teachers alike. They merit, therefore, the urgent attention of foreign language methods course instructors. I believe that if foreign language education courses focus on extensive planning, careful development of materials and organization of program structure, candidate-teachers can learn to develop and participate in successful individualized foreign language programs.

The training of graduate assistants occupies an important part of the professional vitality of foreign language education, and the reasons for this assertion will be given in this chapter. Foreign language training programs for graduate assistants are not and should not be replicas of those courses offered to undergraduates. This claim is supported by many factors to be set forth here. It does not assume that there are no similarities between graduate and undergraduate assistants' training. The discussion/observation/participation format which Busse initiated for her methods outline serves equally well for the training of graduate assistants.

Because the graduate assistant may take his training in a wide variety of circumstances (during his first year of graduate study, with or without prior student teaching, after completing several years of graduate study, etc.) the format of the program varies widely according to local conditions. Rather than discuss those possible formats as preliminary to considerations of content, I have chosen to begin with a discussion of the differences and similarities between high school and undergraduate teaching, for it is on the basis of those comments that colleges and universities must ultimately rest their justification for offering such courses to previously prepared teachers. The graduate assistants for whom these courses are intended present such a heterogeneous group that the question "*who will take the course and why?*" merits careful scrutiny. Treatment of special

---

# 6

# Training Graduate Assistants in Foreign Languages

73          *JEAN-PIERRE BERWALD*

concerns related to the teaching of undergraduates offers further material for this chapter.

The observation segment specifies the various formats of graduate assistant training, the diversity of which may pinpoint the most noteworthy difference between training on the two levels. Pre-semester workshops, regular courses for credit and visitation/sharing arrangements establish the day-to-day routine in which graduate assistants learn as much or more than they do in traditional training programs. In fact, many graduate assistants participate in teaching in a specific area long before they have covered that point in their training sequence, so that observation is at the same time self-evaluation and observation of seasoned colleagues.

The participation section of the chapter concentrates on components of the training program which graduate assistants might find of practical use in carrying out their tasks. My purpose in this section centers on the practical and the immediate, and implies neither that those criteria are the only criteria nor that they deserve less than careful study in undergraduate foreign language education.


## DISCUSSION

What is a graduate assistant? A graduate assistant (or a teaching assistant or a teaching fellow) usually is a candidate for a master's or doctorate degree who earns his tuition and a stipend (typically between $2500 and $4000 a year) by teaching one or more courses or sections of courses. Often he has had little or no teaching experience prior to assuming his responsibilities, as is the case with younger graduate assistants. However, more seasoned graduate assistants may have ample classroom and administrative backgrounds, as well as impressive travel and study abroad. A third category of graduate assistants consists of native speakers who present a wide gamut of teaching potentials with which most graduate assistant coordinators will have had contact.

All people in this wide range of accomplishment have individual ultimate goals—will they end their educations with attainment of an M.A., or will they likely continue on to obtain the doctorate? Those with masters probably will remain at the high school or junior college level; undergraduate and sometimes purely graduate teaching typically will attract holders of the doctorate. Of equal importance is previous training: many M.A. candidates have already completed their certification requirements and nonetheless are compelled to complete the training program, while Ph.D. aspirants may have by-passed the certification procedure.

Arising from this almost bewildering array of students is the methods instructor's question: how can neophyte language teachers learn to provide rich and satisfying learning experiences to a group of undergraduates, many of whom are taught exclusively by graduate assistants in their lower level courses and who finish their language training by completing the degree requirement? In an era of vanishing requirements and declining enrollments in the traditionally taught languages, the matter becomes all the more crucial, since graduate assistants must be able to develop and teach alternative non-major and major curricula. In our large colleges and universities, methods instructors and graduate coordinators must alert graduate assistants to their responsibility to innovate, a task which falls to mature senior faculty in smaller institutions.

Because graduate assistants devote a preponderant amount of their time to the courses in which they are students, the methods instructor must clarify a general perspective of the role of the graduate assistant in undergraduate education as a whole and his enviable place within the department due to daily contact with native speakers, and fruitful discussion of both pedagogical and cross-cultural import. In this area of interpersonal association, the graduate assistant has an agreeable opportunity which his undergraduate counterpart (often the lone student teacher of foreign languages in a school) could rarely hope to duplicate. In addition, graduate assistants discuss problems and insights with peers and superiors on an almost hourly basis because they teach sections of the same courses, with the same texts, quizzes, and often the same marking procedures. The intelligent training program encourages the exchanges and provides for them on a routine basis, for the post-degree years too seldom afford such pleasant and helpful opportunities.

Just as being an instructor at the college level has special characteristics that set it apart from being a high school teacher, actual classroom teaching, too, presents attributes of its own. To many observers, teaching a foreign language is always the same with slight variation due to the ages of the students; in that view there surely is some truth. But, similarly, one is pressed to fault the attitude that college students are a separate breed with heightened personal and political insight that may or may not lead to responsible, enthusiastic classroom performance. For the sake of argument, let us enumerate some aspects of the teaching of undergraduates that might support the position that college teaching of foreign languages really differs from high school teaching.

First, we might think of numbers; in departments which employ graduate assistants there are multi-section courses which necessitate some standardization of approach and methods to allow students to follow a coherent and reasonably planned course of study. Methods instructors must present this issue as a fact of life to graduate assistants, to whom, after all, these multi-section courses are a livelihood.

The other side of the numbers issue involves great potential for individualization, both to meet teacher and student needs and abilities. Whether individualization follows a "track" system or encompasses a self-paced approach, the presence of significant numbers of interested students argues for a close look at individualized instruction within the framework of the methods course. One way of teaching about individualized instruction that I find helpful is to teach my students (with the help of a native speaker) a "new" foreign language. This personal experience usually accounts for more learning than lectures are likely to put across.

Another factor brings resources from outside the college into play. Departments which staff lower level courses with graduate assistants commonly exist in urbanized population centers with sizable segments of native speakers both in the department and in the larger community. Resources beyond the means of most high schools flourish in college towns, and graduate assistants should use these to benefit their classes. Touring drama companies, dance troupes, musical attractions and symposia can enrich the curriculum of surrounding high schools. Such events enhance the teaching of foreign languages and allow graduate assistants to keep abreast of their secondary colleagues' activities.

Time is an often cited difference regarding the teaching practices in college and high school. A common concern in cooperative dramatic performances involves the fear that campus attractions are beyond the comprehension of most high school students with two or three years' training. The recent growth of intensive courses at the secondary level may allay that fear, as the "two years equal one" attitude becomes a thing of the past. In regard to this changing time factor, the graduate assistant methods program should give high priority to high school programs and their results. In few areas of cooperation does there seem to be as much misunderstanding as exists about the question, "what do the schools cover during the year?" Professionalism could receive no more welcome nudge from the methods course than a rapprochement between secondary and undergraduate foreign language teachers on the issue of what should be covered in any term of a total program.

Attitude toward experimentation may serve to characterize college and high school teaching. While size and resources may be stimulating in themselves, many innovative programs stem from secondary institutions while fewer appear to result from experimentation at the college level. Sheer size might be conceived as an obstacle to innovation, but another factor may account for colleges' seemingly conservative approach to change—namely, that good teaching receives more attention from secondary principals and department chairmen than from deans and federal granting agencies at precisely those institutions which employ the most graduate assistants. Hiring practices, for example, normally do not take into account the years spent in graduate assistant teaching toward years of experience in salary and tenure negotiations at the college level.

Finally, undergraduate teaching may differ most from high school teaching because of the very presence of those graduate assistants. Most of them teach with little experience, yet they often devote more time and care to their students than some tenured faculty colleagues. Undergraduates frequently comment that the foreign language class is the one where they are known by their names and where they receive the personal attention of the instructor. One would not generalize from this impression to all graduate assistants, but proponents of affective education in foreign language teaching might well find sympathetic comrades among those graduate assistants alleged to be least qualified to take charge of classroom instruction.

Discussion in the graduate assistant program might, then, center on several issues that could distinguish secondary from college teaching. That college students are older and often freed from parental supervision is obviously one determining factor; second, the teaching of graduate assistants may reveal a certain kind of freshness (or awkwardness) and personal warmth that many undergraduates appear to appreciate. The next sections on observation and participation will investigate freshness and personal warmth, admirable qualities in any teacher at any level, and demonstrate how these attributes may be backed up by sophisticated techniques and competent execution. If the methods sequence occurs just prior to the beginning of the semester, one could argue that this personal dimension could predominate in class discussion at some point in preference to more abstract matters of testing theory and applied linguistics.

## OBSERVATION

Here I consider classroom techniques practiced in the classes of able colleagues whom the graduate assistant observes. The advantage in graduate training is the common authorized text used by all instructors of the same course, as opposed to the variety of texts which undergraduate student teachers may use when they finish their methods course. Methods instructors may choose insofar as possible to synchronize their methods/observation segment with the textbook in actual use.

Graduate assistants automatically observe during their training sequence, because they are normally taking their training while teaching their courses. The methods coordinator should realize the full potential of these circumstances, to the envy of the undergraduate methods instructor who typically sends his student teachers out after they complete the methods course and sees them for three or four all-too-short visitations. While the graduate may feel somewhat frenzied about teaching while learning to teach, the combination of theory and practice which he enjoys should compensate his feelings of being harried.

The possibilities of structuring the graduate assistant training program are numerous; what I have been calling a "methods course" may, in reality, take on a quite different approach from the usual undergraduate methods course. Five such formats will be described below without elaboration of the obvious variations which are possible by combining aspects of any or all of them.

### Pre-semester workshop

The pre-semester workshop is an expedient means of training graduate assistants. Of a few days' length, the workshop usually consists of a number of demonstrations—presentations by "model" instructors. These presentations are useful when done in person because the graduate assistant is placed in the role of student and can determine to some extent the effectiveness of teaching devices. Videotaped presentations provide glimpses of efficient and less efficient teachers. Perhaps the most helpful aspect of any workshop is peer-teaching followed by videotaped critiques. Videotape facilitates training in two other distinct ways: the tapes can be replayed in class and stopped at appropriate times for class comment; they can be viewed by the participant at his convenience, when he can study his strong and weak points. DeLorenzo (1971) suggests using videotape in a laboratory arrangement for viewing demonstrations as well as for recording small-group peer-teaching. His proposal would allow the workshop director to save time in class by playing back perfect presentations for review and critique. The instructor can identify what he approves of in specific terms with appropriate theoretical justification.

### Pre-semester orientation session

The pre-semester orientation session, when the coordinator spends two or three hours giving graduate assistants a detailed set of instructions on technical class and administrative business, requires less time than the pre-semester workshop and avoids extra unpaid workdays. The Ohio State University program provides a standard daily lesson plan for each graduate assistant which is discussed in the orientation session. The plan includes these guidelines:

1.  the schedule of various activities in the lesson plan accounts for the entire class period;

2.  quizzes and tests distributed at the beginning of the term are to be used as scheduled for the rest of the term;

3.  sections must follow the term-long schedule on a day-by-day basis to assure proper coverage of material and to facilitate section changes;

4.  the lesson plans are organized so as to acquaint graduate assistants with basic techniques of foreign language teaching.

Thus the lesson plans offer advice and routine suggestions at a time when most graduate assistants devote the bulk of their time to their own classes. As might be expected, graduate assistants with prior teaching experience may resent this type of arrangement since they are forced to adopt techniques which they may consider inappropriate to their teaching style or temperament.

In addition to disseminating instructions and lesson plans, graduate assistants continue the orientation session by sitting in on classes given by mature instructors, especially at the very beginning of the academic term. Graduate assistants observe model classes daily for a two-week period and are expected to conduct their own classes according to what they have observed. After these initial weeks, graduate assistants are invited to observe classes from time to time whenever new teaching procedures are being introduced. As a part of the program, experienced graduate assistants supervise newcomers several times during the term to critique classes and offer assistance. The press of term papers and course requirements makes these arrangements problematical, however, so that a credit course often seems to be a valuable alternative type of training program.

## Graduate methods courses

Special full-time courses in methods and/or applied linguistics provide a thorough review of theoretical and practical issues under more systematic and sustained conditions than the workshop or the orientation session. Graduate assistants have "live" students to teach every day and are available for routine daily consultation with their colleagues. A major disadvantage of this procedure is that students may not derive maximum benefit from their newly acquired knowledge until the following term. More immediately, the necessarily piecemeal nature of this format may delay the discussion of topics which graduate assistants require early in their teaching duties. In addition, a very full graduate curriculum may not permit an extra course in the schedule.

## Undergraduate methods courses

Staffing problems often make a special graduate assistant methods course impractical, so that regularly offered undergraduate teaching preparation courses (for graduate credit) may be expedient. While some mature graduate assistants might find discussion less knowledgeable than they would wish, assistants often supplement classwork by assisting regular faculty members. Such experience might involve preparing and grading tests, conducting grammar drills and conversation units, supervising work on activity packets, preparing and monitoring laboratory exercises and handling registration chores.

## Weekly seminars

Various features of the above formats may combine to constitute a weekly one-hour seminar/practicum during which demonstration and presentations are offered; problems receive the combined attention of all concerned and quizzes and tests are prepared collectively. These weekly meetings may be conducted either as an independent operation or related to semester meetings, the observation of model instructors and traditional methods courses. Graduate assistants often are grouped according to the class they teach so that only immediately relevant matters come under scrutiny. The major advantage of a weekly seminar is its focus on methods, materials and course content to be taught during a particular week. The experienced coordinator can demonstrate how he would present some of the material; he is also in a good position to discuss and contrast teaching devices to foster some feeling of independence among his graduate assistants. When attendance at these seminars is voluntary (as it most likely is) the coordinator faces the problem of regulating individual obligations towards the seminar.

## PARTICIPATION

The immediate concerns of classroom teaching dictate that participation involve preparing materials of great practicality. When graduate assistants are reluctant to undergo training at all, the methods coordinator can justify his course's existence by gearing assignments to the lesson plans distributed by the department. Following is a list of proposed basic techniques and approaches in which graduate assistants should be competent.

## Listening comprehension

The college or university usually is well equipped to provide listening experience, both in class and out. Language laboratories, film series, coffee houses, foreign students, broadcasts and other resources abound. The key to successful work with listening comprehension is student involvement. Fifty minutes spent in a language laboratory responding to pattern drills will outlast most students' patience. But, exercises which require the student to execute certain physical tasks, to make guesses about the nature of visuals, to fill in missing words from song scripts and to perceive cultural values through listening texts will occupy him as profitably as routine pattern drills. Such exercises can be used to create a highly observable measure of listening skills which does not rely exclusively on paper-and-pencil scoring. The methods instructor must remind his class to portray the listening skills as an enduring acquisition in their language work well beyond the initial sound discrimination stages.

## Introducing a dialogue

The graduate assistant learns to introduce a dialogue by modeling each line several times and calling for choral repetition, in turn followed by individual responses as he moves around the class in order to hear and be heard by everyone. A simple visual aid renders each line more memorable so that subsequent rehearsals require the pictorial stimulus alone; no more than seven to ten minutes per class should be spent in a presentation of this kind. If students appear to be unduly frustrated, additional visuals or a sparing use of the native language will facilitate comprehension. This initial presentation of the dialogue paves the way for later exercises in communicative competence, where the lines are reworked to express ideas that relate to students' lives, while remaining within the structural limits of the dialogue.

## Introducing grammar in speaking

The graduate assistant teaches a point of grammar by proceeding from the known to the unknown, either by mime or by alluding to points of grammar previously taught. For instance:

| *Known* | | *Unknown* |
|---|---|---|
| C'est un livre | > | C'est le livre de Robert etc. |
| Das ist gut | > | Das ist nicht gut etc. |

The graduate assistant follows the oral presentation by asking students if they can formulate the grammar point in their own words. When this has been done, students can apply that rule orally to a number of unfamiliar sentences.

## Teaching grammar in writing

Teaching written grammar has long been the most essential aspect of a foreign language class, often to the exclusion of the development of affective or cultural goals. Traditional means of grammar teaching include homework exercises, worksheets and dictations. One way for the graduate assistant to teach grammar is to appeal to his students' rule-generating abilities: when presented with some sentence transformations, the students write their own rules. A simple transformation in French might be:

> Elle a pris la lettre   >   Elle l'a prise
>
> Elle a mis la table   >   Elle l'a mise

Such inductive teaching of grammar allows the student to explain in simple, nontechnical terminology what has happened to *la lettre* and to *la table* and why *pris* and *mis* take a pronounced final "*e*." The logical follow-up to this technique is for the graduate assistant to give students a worksheet containing sentences to transform that are similar to the ones they had previously analyzed.

## Pattern practice

The graduate assistant needs to learn to conduct pattern practice drills. Pattern practice is a briskly paced exercise of five or six phrases or sentences designed to encourage automatic student manipulation of structure. Drills should be short and limited in number, but they need not be limited to mechanical parroting common to the audio-lingual advocates for whom choral repetition played a preponderant role in class recitation. The choral pattern drill still may have its place in contemporary foreign language teaching, but the individual free response pattern drill represents a step toward real communicative competence.

## Pronunciation practice

During every class hour the graduate assistant should devote about three to five minutes to pronunciation. He need not detail how the foreign language consonants and vowels differ from those of the first language, but differences can be touched upon briefly with examples. A phoneme may be defined by pronouncing it as it occurs in a number of orthographic combinations: "cough," "fish," "phoneme," "eau," "pot," and "aux." Another effective way of presenting phonemes is by means of monolingual and interlingual minimal pairs. With monolingual pairs, the target language is used to contrast two sounds that must be pronounced differently if they are to account for separate meanings:

| | |
|---|---|
| pero | perro |
| rue | roue |
| wash | watch (to Spanish-speaking learners of English) |
| ship | sheep (to French-speaking learners of English) |

Interlingual minimal pairs are used to contrast similar target language and native language phonemes.

| *German* | *French* | *Spanish* |
|---|---|---|
| dir/dear | pire/pier | flora/Flora |
| Haus/house | pour/poor | plaza/plaza |

## Reading

In the early stages of an elementary foreign language, it is preferable that students read material that they have already listened to or recited. In later stages, when they begin to read unfamiliar passages, the graduate assistant's guidance becomes invaluable, as much for facilitating reading comprehension of increasingly uncontrolled texts as well as for the oral skills necessary for the discussion of that material in the foreign language. There are three dimensions in the preparation of reading materials that the graduate assistant must consider: vocabulary presentation, preparation of questions and reading for comprehension.

Once structural patterns are at a level commensurate with the level of reading material, vocabulary presentation becomes an important adjunct in developing reading comprehension. The instructor takes two types of words or expressions out of context: (1) difficult, confusing or low-frequency vocabulary whose explanation would greatly aid in the comprehension of the reading passage; (2) high-frequency, useful vocabulary that students should be held responsible for. The vocabulary in the second category should be taught by means of synonyms, antonyms and examples in a number of contextual situations (Dale et al., 1971). These words and expressions serve as an excellent vehicle for teaching and reviewing grammar. They also lend themselves well to personalizing material and encouraging "real" conversation.

The preparation of questions might center on three types of exercise: sentence fill-ins may convey factual information and yet require key words to be inserted; true-false statements may be assessed as to their veracity and the false items might be rewritten to parallel the story line; important vocabulary items may be used in sentences to illustrate students' knowledge of the manner in which the word fits the overall story line.

Reading for comprehension without recourse to the native language relies on a combination of skills, both lexical and syntactic. Word derivation, inference and paragraph structure typical of writing in the foreign language are areas which the graduate assistant will want to handle with ease as he teaches classes at the second and third year levels.

## The teaching of writing

The first stage in teaching students to write a foreign language is to have them copy work they have already done orally. Class dictation exercises serve to reinforce the writing skill by means of the auditory skill. The graduate assistant should make a habit of dictating four or five familiar sentences that are not too long, or else he can make up a few sentences based on material already covered in class. The dictated sentences are written by students seated or at the board; corrections can be made immediately. The graduate assistant can also ask students to alter the sentences, to form questions based on them and to change tenses; much of this work can be done in the laboratory if class time is too limited.

Dehydrated or telegraphic sentences reinforce writing skills most effectively. The instructor gives students a string such as "*Jack/Jill/hill/pail/water*" and the students are expected to use their knowledge of grammar to complete the sentence correctly both grammatically and semantically.

Reading and writing are necessarily used in complementary fashion. After a passage has been studied and students have answered questions, the graduate assistant asks for a written résumé based on key words and expressions. Guided composition involves a carefully pre-structured set of instructions that might look like this:

> You write a letter to your friend Carol.
> Tell her you saw "The Fonz" last week.
> Tell her that several people fainted.
> Ask her if she has seen *Tommy* yet.
> Tell her to write soon.
> Sign the letter.

The methods instructor should remind his graduate assistants that this technique should neither degenerate into a translation exercise, nor evolve into a completely free composition before students are ready to handle complex structural patterns.

## Teaching culture

Any language reflects the culture of its speakers and any language is part of the culture of its speakers. This reflection of culture in language is evident in the use of proverbs, idiomatic expressions and vocabulary. One simple example of a culture difference is the French equivalent for the American expression "It's as good as gold" (*"C'est bon comme le pain"*). Evidence of cultural influence is present in dialogue, narrative, gesture, posture, intonation patterns, choice of person spoken to, etc. The graduate assistant should be instructed to scrutinize teaching material for cultural value. Brief discussions on customs, traditions and day-to-day life, whether in English or in the target language, support the contention that learning a foreign language opens the door to another culture. Since the teaching of culture has become a popular topic in professional circles, many teachers have adopted the practice of including a culture capsule in their daily classroom routine.

## Classroom routine

Because new teachers often find a routine the most elusive of teacher behaviors, the methods instructor might suggest various components (such as a daily or weekly culture capsule) of a classroom routine.

1. Spend three to five minutes with students in the foreign language for warm-up; re-entry of grammar points serves to discuss matters of local interest.

2. Give at least one written and one oral quiz per week. Do not neglect oral quizzes; if oral work counts toward the grade, show students how oral performance figures in overall progress.

3. Try not to spend more than ten minutes on any one activity, especially during the first year of language instruction; in going from one activity to another do not neglect continuity but avoid too similar exercises.

4. Short dictations should be given each class period; four or five sentences can be dictated and self-checked using the board or an overhead transparency.

5. Make a special effort to know your students personally; obtain some information about each of them in order to personalize some aspects of language training.

6. Bring in a native speaker to interact with the instructor on topics previously explained to the students; encourage their questions and check their ability to "eavesdrop."

## Individualized instruction

Much is being said and done with individualized instruction. From the vast array of literature, foreign language teachers recognize an essential lesson—that they can individualize any one segment of their routine as well as individualize their entire program. Perhaps the most dramatic means of introducing graduate assistants to the concept of individualized instruction allows them to spend two or three hours learning a new foreign language by an individualized procedure.

In the past my students and I, together with native speaker colleagues, have prepared brief programs in Swahili and Italian. We used dittoed instruction sheets and cassette recorders. The instruction sheets contained dialogues, procedures and written self-tests; the cassettes contained recorded dialogues, listening comprehension exercises, pattern drills, pronunciation drills and self-tests. Not only did the prospective teachers get a good idea of what individualized instruction was all about, but also they were able to devise their own programs of individualized instruction based on the techniques and approaches of the materials they had used. Each student receives copies of all the materials constructed by the rest of the class.

Two significant aspects to recall when these various techniques and approaches are covered are the common goal to move from manipulation to communication which occupies much professional theorizing and the possibilities of team-teaching multiple sections of the same course. Amidst the many responsibilities that graduate students take on, none can be more pressing than to urge undergraduates to simplify their ideas for discussion in the foreign language, even at the risk of reducing complex thought to a series of simple propositions. The second aspect brings into play the many talents and interests that graduate assistants reveal in their classroom performance. Certain colleagues will prefer devoting two weeks to a given play for possible laboratory performance; others will develop an ethnic heritage project involving local resources, and still others will treat the linguistic evolution of the foreign language with some introduction to special terminology and analytical technique. Certainly this diversity responds to some students' needs and fosters creativity among graduate assistants.

## CONCLUSION

Most undergraduate foreign language students are taught by graduate assistants at larger colleges and universities. The training of graduate assistants (involved in their own degree programs) is crucial, for many of them center their ambitions around teaching literature courses and require constant reminders that language courses dominate younger professors' course assignments. One can reasonably assume that the bulk of teacher preparation for undergraduate and graduate foreign language teaching stems from graduate assistant programs.

Throughout this chapter, the role of the methods teacher accentuates his daily contact with graduate assistants in the give-and-take of informal discussion, a source of feedback upon which the instructor can revise his course content. Although the training program takes its primary objectives from the daily responsibilities of the graduate assistant, there is reason to suggest that the training program might assume a larger role in undergraduate and graduate instruction by including some treatment of the teaching of literature and culture. Since graduate assistants traditionally staff the beginning courses in language instruction, their contact with techniques and materials of more advanced levels must often await full-time teaching. Hence the break between immediate duties and long-range objectives can only be bridged by a restructured training sequence or by assigning graduate assistants to upper level courses.

That graduate assistant training differs considerably from undergraduate teacher training originates in the collaboration between coordinator and graduate assistant, an opportunity which the secondary methods instructor is not likely to enjoy. He may well lose contact with his students once they finish student teaching, however assiduously he has supervised and observed them during their internship. Graduate assistants are, for better or worse, under the tutelage of their coordinator during their tenure in the department. If they could receive some instruction in the teaching of courses other than those they teach, their training would fulfill its longer range function as well as its short-term goals in the teaching of undergraduate foreign languages.

In the past few years, a number of articles have dealt with the preparation of graduate assistants, and some of these are given in the reference listing for this chapter at the end of this book.

## INTRODUCTION

In recent years, foreign language teachers have become increasingly dissatisfied with the provisions for language instruction in the schools for non-English home language learners. The common practices have been (a) to discourage such youngsters from enrolling in courses in their home language, (b) to enroll them in advanced home language courses together with non-native students who have already studied that language for a year or more, (c) to place them in a language course for beginners (i.e., their home language) or (d) to establish courses in the various areas of the curriculum taught in the home language.

The first practice establishes the situation that, on the one hand, the public schools are attempting to encourage competence in a second language for those who speak only English, and, on the other hand, are discouraging its retention and development among those who speak that language natively. The second line of action results in non-English home language speakers who are visibly superior to their peers in the oral aspects of the foreign language but who are often dramatically inferior in the reading and writing skills. By the second year of foreign language instruction, the native speaker of English will have covered the sound-symbol relationships basic to the generative skills. Since non-native speakers

# 7

# Preparing Teachers
# for Non-English
# Home Language Learners

87              *MANUEL T. PACHECO*

of the target language enjoy such training from the first year, the native speaker is at a critical disadvantage. The third procedure places the non-English home language speaker in a predicament in which he is assumed not to know his own home language with consequent waste of time and energy on the part of the foreign language teacher and student.

None of these practices recognizes or takes advantage of the fact that non-English home language speakers possess a perfectly good and effective system of oral communication that allows their needs to be met in their sociolinguistic environment. The home language is downgraded in many school settings by virtue of having been judged inferior or not worthy of retention, study or further development. The acquisition of a positive self-image thereby is thwarted as the home language is debased in the traditional academic curriculum.

Widespread attention has been drawn, however, to the fourth alternative which provides special classes for non-English home language students, regardless of age or academic achievement, who are able to understand ordinary conversation in the non-English language with parents and friends. This chapter will deal with the latter alternative in terms of three dimensions pertinent to the methods course:

1.  A rationale and statement of goals will be formulated for the methods instructor.

2.  A treatment of linguistic, cultural, sociological and educational background will brief the prospective teacher.

3.  Suggested activities will be proposed to help teachers acquire both the background and teaching strategy that will contribute to the fulfillment of the goals enumerated in the first part of the course.

Throughout the chapter source references and curricular materials will be cited although the methods instructor should seek documentation regarding the specific home language his methods students will deal with.

## RATIONALE AND STATEMENT OF GOALS

Spanish, French, German, Russian, Portuguese and other languages are taught as foreign languages throughout the United States, even where the population of native speakers outnumbers the English-speaking population. In those areas, it is reasonable to assume that knowing a language other than English is valuable enough to encourage English-speaking students to learn a "foreign" language. The non-English home language speaker should also be persuaded to continue to develop the language skills he has acquired during his informal home education.

The home language of many non-English home language speakers often evolves apart from a standard dialect, so that in foreign language classes (teaching the home language) those speakers face problems not encountered by other beginning foreign language learners. The secondary school years witness a gradual effacement of marked non-standard linguistic traits. Non-native speakers, on the contrary, do not continue to refine their home language; rather, they find that the classroom ignores their home language training in favor of the exclusive use of English. The result is not that the home language is destroyed, but that it takes the course of being diverted into the home and peer groups with a resulting emphasis on highly individualized, less standard and more regional characteristics. The home language is thereby increasingly devalued by the larger English-speaking society.

However, the use of a non-standard dialect does not imply a less effective or inferior system of oral communication. The use of a dialect means that the communication constraints are more evident in terms of social and regional boundaries. Thus, the foreign language methods course emphasizes the positive view of the student's non-native dialect and an understanding of the relationship between a standard and non-standard dialect.

The non-English home language speaker must be assured that, by developing a command of a standard dialect of his home language, he is supporting and enhancing his self-concept. Thus, not only must the foreign language teacher be convinced that the student's dialect is integral to his self-concept, but also he must convince his students of the worth of the home language by focusing systematically and patiently on the relationships between the regional dialect and standard dialect as taught in the classroom situation. Basic to this attitude of the foreign language teacher is his attitude toward the non-English home language speaker, one showing wholehearted acceptance of the student, without censure of or exertion of pressure on the non-standard speaker.

The Texas Education Agency (1970) has proposed a rationale for the non-English home language course which provides the core for methods class discussion:

1.  to encourage the learner to acquire a sense of his own identity as a member of his cultural-linguistic group and to help him contribute to that group's effort towards socio-economic and cultural equality;

2.  to give the learner full command of his home-language resources in appropriate cultural and social settings so that he can realize his full potential as a bilingual person;

3.  to reinforce, through his home language, other areas of the school curriculum in order to expand the learner's knowledge and perspectives in those areas.

Foreign language methods students should consider the means by which these goals may be achieved in the non-English home language course where the affective and the cognitive domains are partners in the educational enterprise. Specific purposes of the non-English home language courses might include these aims:

1. to enable the student to understand one of the various standard dialects of his home language, and to refine his listening skills in order to distinguish between the standard and non-standard dialect;

2. to enable the student to express himself in the standard dialect without recourse to English or non-standard dialect;

3. to enable the student to read the target language with comprehension and enjoyment;

4. to enable the student to write in the target language materials presented orally and/or read on topics within his experience;

5. to enable the student to interpret the home culture and acquire a sense of pride in his heritage;

6. to enable the student to become familiar with opportunities for using the target language in the business, vocational, recreational and educational worlds.

Although many similarities exist between bilingual-bicultural education and alternative 4, it is imperative to point out that there are very basic differences in purposes and methods of instruction. Bilingual education, as commonly understood and designed, has been limited to the elementary school and has as its primary goal the development of common learnings by using the learner's home language to teach the content areas while the English language is being studied. A secondary accessory objective is the retention and further maturing of the student's English. But the fourth alternative proclaims as its primary objective the retention and development of the student's non-English home language with a concomitant reinforcement of the content areas of the curriculum; this alternative usually is elected in junior and senior high school. Thus, bilingual education concentrates on common subject matter and the acquisition of English, while the fourth alternative centers on retaining and refining home-language skills.

The teacher in a bilingual/bicultural program in most states must have a teaching certificate for the elementary school, since the entire elementary curriculum is involved; in addition, the teacher must be bilingual. However, the qualifications of the teacher of the special home language courses described here can be and often are quite different; these qualifications will be outlined in the following section, along with a proposed sequence of methods class activities designed to prepare foreign language teachers to teach non-English home language courses.

## CONTENT, MATERIAL, AND
## PROJECTS FOR THE METHODS COURSE

Teachers of non-English home language courses should expect to contribute to the development of students who can function academically, socially and emotionally in their home language and in the language of the wider population. In order to fill the role adequately the methods teacher must promote an empathetic and respectful attitude on the part of the classroom teacher. In addition, the prospective teacher must be fully competent in the home language and in the local dialect of the home language. Gaarder et al. (1972) have listed additional qualifications for prospective teachers which are adapted for presentation here.

1. He is bicultural; it helps, but is neither necessary nor sufficient, to be born into biculturalism. Feelings are fine, but a foreign language teacher needs some facts about the history, social structure, folkways, values, aspirations and immediate environment of his pupils and their families.

2. He has some knowledge about the nature of language and of language learning, including the theory and application of contrastive linguistics.

3. He has knowledge of the content and methods of teaching in the home language in all areas of the curriculum. Ordinarily this cannot be acquired except by studying in those areas through the medium of the home language. Intensive practice and study in a target language community is an absolute necessity for the prospective teacher. Although many prospective teachers perhaps will prefer to live and study in a country where the target language is the national language, it is also advisable for him to live in a locale in which the dialect under consideration is spoken in order to broaden his contact with speakers and their lives.

Truly bilingual communities (which would lend themselves to the types of preparation recommended above) exist in many parts of the United States. Other of the listed qualifications can be realized as a part of the regular foreign language methods course. Particular care should be exerted that adequate coverage be devoted to material pertinent to the prospective teacher.

## Proposed methods course or unit outline

I. Language and Linguistics—The focus on this portion might take the following points of departure:

    A. the role of the local dialect and its relationship to the standard dialect

    B. a contrastive study of the phonology and syntax of the standard dialect and the home dialect

    C. a contrastive study of the phonology and syntax of the target language and English

    D. Readings for class discussion. It would be expected that the third item would be a normal part of the regular methods course, so that little additional time would be required for this activity. Items A and B are dealt with in the following readings:

1. *Teaching Spanish in School and College to Native Speakers of Spanish,* available from the Superintendent of Documents, U.S. Government Printing Office, Washington, D.C. 20402, which can also be consulted in the October 1972 issue of *Hispania,* pp. 619-631. Although this pamphlet deals exclusively with Spanish, the approach is suited to all languages. (For French, see G. Brault, 1961. "Comment doit-on enseigner le français aux jeunes franco-americains," *Le Canada-Américain 11,* vi: 30-34.

   *AND*

2. *Language as a Lively Art,* by Ray Past (Dubuque: Wm. C. Brown, 1970, pp. 252-276). In the chapter entitled "What is 'English' Anyhow?" Past introduces the nature of language, the development of dialects and the relationships of regional and social dialects to standard dialect.

   *AND*

3. "Local Standards and Spanish in the Southwest" by J. Donald Bowen in *Studies in Language and Linguistics, 1970-71* (R. Ewton and J. Ornstein, eds.) (El Paso: Texas Western/University of Texas Press, 1971). Bowen makes a convincing case for the legitimacy of Southwestern United States Spanish, as well as describing some of its phonological, syntactic and lexical characteristics.

   *OR*

4. Phillip D. Ortego, 1971. "The Chicano Renaissance," *Social Casework 52,* v: 294-307 (issue subtitled "La Causa Chicana"); and "Linguistics and the Disadvantaged," by Clemens L. Hallman in (Fogan, Edward R. ed.) *English and the Disadvantaged* (Scranton: International Textbook Co., 1967) deal with ethnic and non-standard dialects.

   *OR*

5. Several chapters in Kelly, L. G., ed., *Description and Measurement of Bilingualism* (Toronto: University of Toronto Press, 1969), are appropriate for descriptions of Puerto Rican Spanish.

   *OR*

6. Other relevant articles which contrast the regional dialect with a standard dialect.

II. Culture

   A. Teacher Attitude—Many non-native speakers of English experience culture clashes between their home culture and the dominant culture. In many cases, foreign language teachers expect these students to exhibit the cultural characteristics of the dominant group because of a lack of basic knowledge of divergent cultural norms in the target language community. It is imperative that prospective teachers be aware of the cultural constructs among the target population and recognize that these students will probably span the range between cultural polarities. It is important, then, to assign readings that will identify characteristics of the target community; these characteristics must be consequently portrayed as acceptable patterns in their own right and legitimate alternate behavior patterns.

B.    Source Materials—In order to maximize the distribution of information, foreign language methods instructors and prospective teachers should familiarize themselves with relevant journals and ERIC entries of potential interest to the methods class (Andersson and Boyer, 1970).

III.   Curriculum and Methods

A.    Curriculum—According to a report (Gaarder et al., 1972) of the American Association of Teachers of Spanish and Portuguese concerning the teaching of Spanish to native speakers of Spanish, home language courses should consist of three elements:

1.    selective reinforcement of other areas of the school curriculum
2.    history and culture of the learner's people
3.    Spanish language development

(These recommendations might apply to other languages as well.)

B.    Method—It is assumed that the home language will be better and more easily learned as an incidental, unavoidable facet of school life than as an end in itself. Therefore these courses reinforce the curriculum; they do not displace any part of it.

1.    Prospective teachers should consider basic teaching strategies for the various subject matter disciplines which they will teach in the target language. Methods courses might study teachers' manuals to popular texts, or they might invite local specialists to present "bird's-eye" summaries of teaching approaches; pre-service and in-service observations would complement these projects.

2.    Students with inadequate command of the target language must be given exercises similar to those current in foreign language teaching practices.

3.    Suggestions from Gaarder et al. (1972) indicate that
    a.    the teacher's positive and supportive attitude is crucial;
    b.    the teacher's command of the language must be excellent and conversational;
    c.    practice and comprehension may be facilitated by:
        (1)    teacher awareness of the language he is using and how the learner receives the language

<ol start="2">
<li>(2) frequent paced introduction of new vocabulary and expressions</li>
<li>(3) frequent use of paraphrase and inference by both teacher and student</li>
<li>(4) exercises in written and oral conversation from standard dialect to regional/social dialects and vice versa</li>
<li>(5) broad use of media portraying regional variants of speech and assessment of these variants and their meaning</li>
<li>(6) hearing practice in the identification of the country of origin of home language speakers through recordings of their speech</li>
</ol>

d. the two languages in question should be kept separate at all times during the process of language development; while some ethnic literature employs two languages simultaneously, this ability is not a priority for most students.

4. The AASTP seven-step strategy (Gaarder et al., 1972) should be the object of micro-lessons during the methods class; the strategy is included here for assistance in preparing materials. *The Seven-Step Strategy.* In the classroom a good learning strategy to develop literacy and discrimination (even if the teacher has little command of Spanish) is the following. High school students can use it individually and with little guidance.

a. Pupil learns quite easily from the teacher the basic orthography of Spanish by recognition of Spanish words on the chalkboard and simple directions. This takes only a few class periods.

b. He tape-records an original statement of any kind (very short at first) then transcribes his own statement. The teacher checks the transcription (and might learn something in the process) but does not criticize either syntax or lexicon. Pupil does it over (listening to his words played back) and learns to do an accurate transcription. All final transcriptions are kept in a bound notebook. Pupil then shows that he can read aloud accurately his transcription.

c. The exercise is repeated many times with longer and more varied original statements. The pupil is learning to read and write.

d. Pupil also learns (without ceasing to work with original statements and accounts) to transcribe and then read aloud short passages recorded by other speakers of

Spanish. He is learning to read and write other kinds of Spanish.

e.  Pupil later reads short statements, bits of conversation, etc., from books or newspapers, hides the selection from sight and records his own version of it, i.e., "telling what he reads." He then transcribes exactly his version and thus has two perfectly legitimate variant forms of the same thing. This powerful exercise should be used many times to develop a sense of the difference between the two. There is no need for invidious comparisons or value judgments by the teacher. The pupil unaided sees and hears the similarities and differences clearly enough.

f.  The two versions of every exercise should be copied on facing pages of the bound notebook: the original on the left, the student's version on the right. The exercise material should be chosen for appropriateness of cognitive and linguistic level and, however short or long, should be interesting.

g.  The final step in this process of learning to read and write and perceive differences between two versions of Spanish is for the pupil to read aloud *accurately* the sets of two variant transcriptions and thus demonstrate that he perceives *accurately* the differences between them. This seven-step procedure enables the pupil to learn by himself at his own rate with no expertise required from the teacher except elementary knowledge of sound-letter correspondences in Spanish, plus the time to select appropriate sentences and longer selections for practice material.

IV.  Materials

A.  Sources adaptable for teacher training materials

1.  Texas Education Agency, 1970. *Espanol para alumnos hispanohablantes* (Austin). (Also available: ERIC: ED 047588). Intended to guide high school speakers in setting up special classes for Spanish speakers.

2.  Fuentes, Irma et al., 1970. *Spanish for Spanish-Speaking Students.* Brooklyn: New York City Board of Education, N.Y. Bureau of Curriculum Development. (Also available: ERIC: ED 051681)

3.  Gaarder, Bruce et al., 1972. *Teaching Spanish in School and College to Native Speakers of Spanish* (U.S. Department of Health, Education and Welfare. Superintendent of Documents. U.S. Government Printing Office, Washington, 20402). Also published in *Hispania 55* (Oct. 1972): 619-631.

4. Barker, Marie Esman, 1971. *Español para el bilingue.* Skokie (Ill.): National Textbook Company.

B. Additional sources
1. U.S. Department of Agriculture. U.S. Government Printing Office, Superintendent of Documents, Washington, 20402. Pamphlets written in clear, simple language, mostly in Spanish, dealing with consumer education; appropriate for use in Home Economics, etc.
2. Stechert-Hafner, Inc., 31 East 10th Street, New York 10003. How-to-do-it books, in Spanish, dealing with art activities, small motor repair, child rearing, sewing, hobbies, geology, household repairs, children's games.
3. *Materials en Marcha para el esfuerzo bilingue-bicultural.* ESEA Title VII, San Diego City Schools, 2950 National Avenue, San Diego, California 92213. Excellent source of materials developed in Spansih- and Portuguese-speaking countries.
4. Dissemination Center for Bilingual Bicultural Education, 6504 Tracor Lane, Austin, Texas 78721. This office regularly releases and sells new and extremely valuable curriculum guides and bibliographies.

## CONCLUSION

As minority populations increase in numbers and in political representation, properly prepared non-English home language instructors will be required to staff the growing programs across the United States. The preceding outline might serve as a basic proposal for a course devoted to home language curriculum and instruction, or for a specialized unit within a general methods course.

The teaching of foreign languages has been for many decades centered on the English-speaking child whose foreign linguistic heritage was thought to constitute an obstacle to effective and efficient schooling. Two generations ago, students who spoke a second language were thought by teachers to qualify for remedial help. At school, these children were coerced into abandoning the use of their home languages.

The presence of many non-native speakers of English in numerous regions of the United States has brought about a reassessment of the role of the home language in the school curriculum. Less and less is the home language considered a hazard to public education or a stigma on social standing. Students can now participate in special programs designed to further their knowledge of that language through curricula taught in the home language covering the standard range of subject matter disciplines required for accreditation purposes. These programs attempt to reinforce pride in the ethnic heritage and dialect via language consciousness. Large cities are obligated to provide bilingual policemen, telephone repairmen, medical personnel, etc.

Aside from the worthy social purposes proclaimed for these non-English educational programs, traditional foreign language courses find a corollary advantage in the preservation and cultivation of our ethnic linguistic heritage. For non-native speakers of Spanish or French, to take but two common examples, the study of a foreign language takes on a new dimension when that foreign language is spoken in everyday situations perhaps a few miles distant from the classroom. No longer do foreign language classes concentrate on transoceanic voyages and touristic images of target cultures; rather, the target culture or a variety of it is frequently an accepted fact of local community life. As a result we foreign language teachers must seek to abandon the worn tradition that asserts Castilian Spanish as *the* dialect suitable for classroom use. Vestiges of the French colonial presence in black Africa take on new life when black foreign language students study the French language and culture as they have evolved in black Africa. This growing awareness of "non-standard" dialects stems, in part at least, from our non-English home language programs in the United States.

The methods course will be required to develop a generation of teachers familiar with the issues and techniques appropriate to classes concerned with retaining and developing the non-English home language and other areas of the curriculum which are taught in the non-English home language. Because the implications of non-English home language courses and curricula are not yet fully absorbed into our notions of public education, these courses must present the issues in their broadest academic and social senses.

This final chapter focuses upon three central concerns which can be said to underlie the nature, objectives and scope of the methods course. These concerns are:

1. insight into historical and theoretical backgrounds of language teaching;

2. implementation of classroom techniques derived from these backgrounds;

3. familiarity with opportunities for professional growth.

The methods instructor will select a proper blend of material from these chapters according to his own experience and that of his students. Uppermost in his mind is the compelling need to focus his teaching on the realities of the upcoming student teaching experience. His classroom lectures and projects will dwell upon those topics not suitably clarified by available materials. Readings, however, will be a principal source of information.

This chapter will review the impressive array of materials that the methods teacher has at his disposal. It will be divided in accordance with the three concerns that unite the other chapters of this book.

# 8

# A Methods Teacher's Guide
# to Information Sources

*ALAN GARFINKEL*

# HISTORICAL AND THEORETICAL CONSIDERATIONS

## Historical considerations

Historical considerations are of primary importance most notably in this era when much that is "new" reflects long-standing, if not widely acknowledged, principles of language instruction. A further justification for this area of concern arises in the recurring problem of how we motivate students to continue language study beyond the elementary courses. Lack of familiarity with these backgrounds invites us to repeat failure and ignore successes.

For these two reasons Kelly's book (1969) represents a comprehensive review of foreign language teaching. While Kelly engages our attention with a unique topical organization, Pillet (1974) scans the various changes foreign language study has undergone in the 20th century. Because the pluralism now being advocated encourages us to take for our own the best parts of each method, Méras' guide (1962) serves us best by helping to locate and identify sources which were studiously ignored at the height of the audio-lingual frenzy. A chronological organization furnishes Diller (1971) with a framework for a discussion of the basic principles of empiricist and rationalist theories of second language acquisition.

Each methods teacher derives from these backgrounds an awareness of professional development which pertains to his own epoch and experience. This awareness is healthy so long as it permits one's attention to concentrate as much on the character of the local situation as on the broader scene, to avoid the extremes of bandwagon-type approaches. For it is the nature of the local clientele that historical perspective has proven to be the determining factor in successful language programs.

## Theoretical considerations

Theoretical considerations lead us to examine the rationale for classroom technique. To which works might the methods instructor turn for statements of psychological rationale? Rivers (1968), Chastain (1971), and Jakobovits (1970) delineate theoretical positions which are of immediate interest to methods teachers and students alike. Rivers (ibid.) analyzes audio-lingual methodology through its major psychological foundations. Chastain (ibid.) compares behavioralist and cognitivist theories for their bearing on language teaching practice. Jakobovits (ibid.) fuses psychological and linguistic considerations as he distinguishes between the student's ability to manipulate linguistic structures and his ability to communicate a message.

The degree to which the methods course treats linguistics will be determined by the nature of the courses complementing it. For purposes of introducing students to the science of linguistics the teacher might consult volumes by Moulton (1970) and Politzer (1965; 1968; 1970). Moulton (ibid.) provides a handbook of linguistic advice for adults who wish to learn a second language.

Politzer (ibid.), Politzer and Politzer (1972), and Politzer and Staubach (1965) are contrastive in nature and include a volume of specific advice to the adolescent foreign language learner. Kadler (1970) has written a basic introduction to the science of linguistics. It is not specifically contrastive, and it includes a chapter entitled "A New Look at Grammar." Thomas (1965) presents an explanation and analysis of transformational grammar which could be applied to the teaching of foreign languages.

The prospective teacher's study of the nature of language must continue from applied linguistics to a broader social context especially now when the anthropological view of culture influences our approach to teaching. This view of language in a cultural context, Farb (1974) is one of the most recent to point out, determines the impact of our attempts at communication as much as any other element (e.g., linguistic proficiency).

Theoretical considerations are vital because they set the direction for classroom practice. To set the direction for classroom practice is not, however, to define its final form. While the prospective teacher needs to be exposed to theoretical considerations for purposes of orientation, he should not expect those considerations to be able to shape classroom procedures. The routine demands of the foreign language classroom impede a direct item-for-item extrapolation from theory to the practice of particular methods.

## CLASSROOM PRACTICE: CURRICULUM AND TECHNIQUE

Methods for language teaching are of such importance to the preparation of the foreign language teacher that we tend to speak of that course which provides the bulk of professional orientation as "the methods course," regardless of whatever other topics it may deal with. Prospective teachers will need to consider both *method* in a general sense and specific *methods* for immediate classroom objectives. This consideration enables them to structure teaching so that day-to-day activities form a recognizable whole.

### Methods analysis

To facilitate this generic view of method, Mackey (1965) offers the most comprehensive treatment available. Beginning with applicable elements of psychological and linguistic theory, he indicates the questions we should ask in considering any method. Similarly, Brooks (1964), Dodson (1967), Hester (1970) and Lado (1964) are concerned with the internal cohesiveness of language teaching methods; but each writer advocates the use of a particular method. Rivers (1968) and Grittner (1969) offer an even more comprehensive view of methods course topics by including such factors as classroom management and the establishment of instructional goals. Classroom practice, as it evolves from theoretical considerations, is amply treated by Chastain (1971) in his dual-purpose volume.

From the first day he enters the classroom, the methods instructor is aware of the concern his students have for the label attached to the methodology they are planning to adopt. That is why discussion of methods analysis precedes other topics here. The methods instructor, however, must concern himself first with directing his students' attention to the establishment of an organizational scheme.

## Objectives and directions

The prospective teacher should understand that it is possible to cast the outcomes of his teaching in terms of what his students will be able to do as a result of that teaching. This is not to say that every breath need fit into a behavioral scheme at the cost of transforming students into robots. The methods teacher will find that Valette and Disick (1972) can help prospective teachers to state purposes and expected outcomes so explicitly that any student or colleague will perceive when they have been accomplished. Such a clear statement of objectives is of special importance to programs that place responsibility for learning on the student as much as on the teacher. If only one of these partners in learning has a clear perception of course objectives, the other doubtlessly will work less efficiently than he might. Widely known writers in the field of individualized foreign language instruction, Altman (1972), Altman and Politzer (1971), Grittner and LaLeike (1973) and Logan (1973) lead us to consider making the student our functional partner in learning without insisting on a slavish devotion to a rigid model of individualized instruction. In fact, they warn that a teacher who can honestly report satisfaction with student achievement, motivation, enrollment figures, and his own professional status ought to find out what causes him to do so well and to remain on that successful course. Innovative programs, the creations of successful teachers, have most recently gained attention through the report by Love and Honig (1973), who describe programs at all levels of public school instruction. Levenson and Kendrick (1967) and Donoghue (1967) stress foreign language instruction in the elementary school (FLES).

## Procedures

Professional success, as described above, is the end objective of the methods course. The literature of foreign language teaching documents a wide array of materials in this regard that prospective teachers should be aware of. The most recent and comprehensive treatment of classroom procedures, by Allen and Valette (1972), provides an indispensable guide that teachers and student teachers alike will treasure. Stanislawczyk-Yavener (1976) contributed a welcome compilation of techniques that complement Allen and Valette's earlier work.

Collections of less recent vintage are offered by Huebener (1959; 1960). Methods students in search of games to use for classroom activities find Dorry (1966) a helpful source. Classroom games, of course, enable the student teacher to accomplish several worthy goals aside from mere diversion.

The "skill-getting" activities which must precede many games are detailed by Etmekjian (1966) for French teachers. His procedures remain applicable for use in learning other foreign languages. Stack (1971) also provides various kinds of "skill-getting" pattern drills along with guidelines for the maintenance and management of language laboratories while the differing physical arrangements for library-style and classroom oriented language laboratories are outlined by Hocking (1967).

## CULTURE

Morain, in the present volume, has provided one of the most comprehensive guides to the teaching of cultural concepts and patterns presently available. Methods instructors will want their students to know about the teaching devices she presents. Lafayette's chapter in a volume edited by Grittner (1974a) ties the presentation of cultural patterns to the formation of an individualized program, and Jenks, writing in another volume edited by Grittner (1974b), proposes a strategy for leading students to draw their own cultural hypotheses. The sociocultural context is related to the teaching of foreign languages and literatures by Nostrand (1974). The newness of the teaching of everyday cultural patterns generates two problems for methods teachers and their students: what to teach, and how to teach it. Available literature deals more with the latter than the former; but recent interdisciplinary efforts (Hamilton, 1973) are likely to yield increasingly valuable sources of new information.

### Testing

As goals set directions for teaching programs, tests and quizzes act as instruments to determine the extent to which teaching strategies have contributed to the fulfillment of those goals. Prospective teachers will need information on how to design these instruments and how to interpret the data they yield. Valette's handbook (1967) is designed to help teachers devise sound procedures for measurement to determine the outcomes of teaching. A principal advantage of her presentation is its matter-of-fact, nontechnical mode of explanation. While Lado's presentation (1961) similarly sets out to enable language teachers to gather empirical evidence of achievement, his mode of explanation presumes some knowledge of technical measurement procedures on the part of the reader. Two kinds of tests, measures of aptitude and attitude, often given insufficient attention in teacher preparation are covered by Jakobovits (1970) and Pimsleur and Quinn (1971).

The cornerstone of the methods teacher's discussion of testing must be the direct relationship between the setting of objectives and the formation of tests and quizzes (evaluation). In other words, the methods instructor must repeatedly admonish his students to adhere to the principle, "Test what you teach and teach what you test." Audio-visual aids for the methods class can help achieve that goal.

## Audiovisual aids in methods courses

*Note. The numbers in parentheses are references given at the end of this section.*

The Educational Testing Service's multi-media kit (7), *Modern Languages: Teaching and Testing*, amplifies the importance of the role of testing using a filmstrip, tape and workbook. The kit is also a promotional device for the *MLA Cooperative Tests*,, and, therefore, is made available at a minimal charge.

Interaction analysis is a system for observing teacher and pupil behavior in the classroom. It classifies behaviors observed into groups to enable teachers to get a dependable measure of how often the teacher dominates classroom proceedings and how often students are given an opportunity to contribute to the class. The system does not purport to evaluate teaching directly. It only provides information to be examined in the light of a statement of classroom goals. Such an examination can enable teachers to see how well their stated goals are realized by the behaviors observed in their classes. Moskowitz' multi-media kits (13, 14) offer training in a method of interaction analysis especially suited to foreign language teaching.

Methods students always search for a rationale for the study of languages to present to their students. The American Association of Teachers of French offers a recent filmstrip (1) addressed to junior high school students. The American Council on the Teaching of Foreign Languages also offers a filmstrip (3) dealing with all languages. However, some of the facts and figures it provides are no longer applicable.

The widest range of audiovisual materials available for the methods class are those which show a particular method in use. The best known of these were produced when audio-lingual methods were being discussed in NDEA workshops. The Capretz films (6) show audio-lingual techniques in use in French, German, Russian and Spanish. The Center for Applied Linguistics films (10) present linguistic and psychological theoretical bases and classroom practice from a behavioralistic viewpoint. Both series retain their value for comparative purposes. Asher, known as the developer of the "total physical response" approach, shows his system in action in films entitled "Demonstration of a New Strategy in Language Learning" (4) and "Strategy for Second Language Learning" (5). The Northeast Conference on the Teaching of Foreign Languages has produced films (17, 18, 19) dealing with teaching procedures and the use of audiovisual aids. At least two textbook publishing companies have currently available films showing their texts in use. Houghton Mifflin offers *"Spanish for Communication* Demonstration Films" (8) and the Encyclopedia Britannica Educational Corporation offers "Teaching French with Films" (9). The commercial purposes of these films and many others like them do not negate their value for the methods course. "Techniques for Teaching German" (15) is a series of ten teaching demonstrations with commentaries in English. The 65-minute film stresses both cognitive and behavioral aspects of language teaching while it places special emphasis on using the target language almost exclusively. It is also available on videotape. In addition, the American Association of Teachers of French offers a recently produced film regarding methods of teaching French (2); and an inexpensive multi-media kit (11) presents data on how to use the single most important resource for the professional growth of the prospective language teacher, the ERIC system.

## Audiovisual Materials

1. American Association of Teachers of French. "Why Study French?" Champaign (Ill.): 1973. *(filmstrip—cassette—tape)*.

2. American Association of Teachers of French. "Focus on French" Champaign (Ill.): 1974. (Film available from Daniel J. Maillet, 75 Meadow St., Garden City, Long Island, New York 11530.)

3. American Council on the Teaching of Foreign Languages. "Why Study Foreign Languages?" New York: MLA/ACTFL Materials Center, 1968. *(filmstrip—tape)*

4. Asher, James J. "Demonstration of a New Strategy in Language Learning" Los Gatos (Cal.): Sky Oaks Productions, 1964. (Film available from Sky Oaks Productions, 19544 Sky Oaks Way, Los Gatos, Cal. 95030.)

5. Asher, James J. "Strategy for Second Language Learning." Los Gatos (Cal.): Sky Oaks Productions, 1972. (Film available from Sky Oaks Productions, 19544 Sky Oaks Way, Los Gatos, Cal. 95030.)

6. Capretz, Pierre J. "Audiolingual Techniques for Teaching Foreign Languages" (NDEA, Title VI, Contract Number 9361) Washington: U.S. Office of Education, 1962—. (Films available from Norwood Films, Washington, D.C. and Indiana University, Audio-visual Center, Bloomington, Ind. 47401.)

7. Cooperative Test Division, Educational Testing Service. Princeton (N.J.): Educational Testing Service. *(filmstrip—tape)*

8. Cruz-Salvadores, José Manuel. "Spanish for Communication Demonstration Film" Los Angeles: University of California at Los Angeles, Department of Spanish. *(film)*

9. Encyclopaedia Britannica, 1966. "Teaching French with Films" Chicago: Encyclopaedia Britannica. (Film available from the Encyclopaedia Britannica Educational Corporation, 425 North Michigan Avenue, Chicago, Ill. 60611.) Part I: Listening and Speaking; Part II: Reading and Writing.

10. Ferguson, Charles A. *Principles and Methods of Teaching a Second Language* (Five motion pictures: "The Nature of Language," "The Sounds of Language," "The Organization of Language," "Words and Their Meanings" and "Modern Techniques in Language Teaching.") Washington, D.C.: Center for Applied Linguistics, 1965. (Films are available from Teaching Film Custodians, 25 West 43d Street, New York 10036.)

11. Lee, Alben. "Introduction to ERIC." "How to Use ERIC." "ERIC Advanced Training Program." Monmouth (Or.): Teaching Research Division of the Oregon State System of Higher Education. (Kit available from The National Audio-visual Center, Washington, D.C. 20409.) *(filmstrip—record)*

12. Minnesota Mining and Manufacturing Co., Inc. (3-M Corporation). "Taking the Mystery Out of the Language Lab." St. Paul, Minn. *(filmstrip—tape)*

13. Moskowitz, Gertrude. "The Foreign Language Teacher Interacts." Minneapolis: Association for Productive Teaching, 1967. (Kit available from Association for Productive Teaching, Room 1268, 5408 Chicago Avenue South, Minneapolis, Minn. 55417.) *(filmstrip—tape)*

14. Moskowitz, Gertrude. "Don't Smile Till Christmas." Minneapolis: Association for Productive Teaching, 1973. (Available from Association for Productive Teaching, 4329 Nicollet Avenue South, Minneapolis, Minn. 55409.) (*filmstrip–tape*)

15. Mueller, Klaus A. "Techniques for Teaching German" Berkeley: University of California, 1970. (Film available from the Educational Television Office, 5 Dwinelle Hall, University of California, Berkeley, Cal. 94720.)

16. National Association of Educational Broadcasters. "A Word in Your Ear." Minneapolis (Minn.): 3-M Corporation, 1968.

17. Northeast Conference. "Bonjour tout le Monde." Middlebury (Vt.): Northeast Conference, 1970. (Film available from the Northeast Conference, P.O. Box 623, Middlebury, Vt. 05753.)

18. Northeast Conference. "Media in Foreign Language Teaching," "Media in French Language Teaching," "Media in German Language Teaching," "Media in Spanish Language Teaching." Middlebury (Vt.): Northeast Conference, 1970. (Films available from the Northeast Conference, P.O. Box 623, Middlebury, Vt. 05753.)

19. Northeast Conference. "Romani Viventes et Dicentes" Middlebury (Vt.): Northeast Conference, 1970. (Film available from the Northeast Conference, P.O. Box 623, Middlebury, Vt. 05753.)

## PROFESSIONAL OUTREACH

The most comprehensive and up-to-date methods course has failed its clientele unless it has encouraged them to begin a career-long search for new stimuli to professional growth. Certainly such experiences as attending a summer workshop contribute to professional growth. But on-the-spot refinement of teaching gains much from contact with other teachers through professional associations and from the reading of journals and other publications.

### Professional organizations for language teachers

In our society, it is common for people who share interests to band together for the purpose of encouraging widespread attention and even allegiance to it, whatever it may be. Many such groups of people have been quite successful in these efforts. Ecologists, consumer information specialists, doctors, lawyers, truck drivers, advocates of career and vocational education, veterans groups, feminists, minority group advocates, . . . to name but a few. If we are ever to do an adequate job of representing the mutual interests of language teachers both to the public and to a significant proportion of teachers themselves, we must begin with language teachers in training. As methods teachers, language teachers, literary critics, and others involved in language teacher training, we ourselves have an obligation to join these professional organizations, to participate in their meetings, to read and submit articles to their journals, and, above all, to encourage our students to join and likewise participate. This section will list some of the organizations for language teachers and make a few points about the benefits they offer to our students.

Organizations shown with an asterisk (*) are among the smaller groups. Many are new and especially deserving of support, because those who teach the heretofore uncommonly taught languages can claim a substantial portion of the credit for any increase in foreign language enrollment that may have occurred in recent years.

### American Association of Teachers of Arabic*
Frederic J. Cadora, Arabic Program, The Ohio State University, Columbus, O. 43210

### American Association of Teachers of French
F. W. Nachtmann, 59 E. Armory Avenue, Champaign, Illinois 61820

The AATF publishes *The French Review,* a journal featuring both pedagogical and literary studies. It sponsors a National Information Bureau, annual meetings, state chapters, a traveling realia exhibit, a national contest for students, an honor society for students, a teacher placement bureau, group flights to France, summer scholarships for teachers, and supplemental publications.

### American Association of Teachers of German
339 Walnut Street, Philadelpha, Pa. 19106

The AATG publishes two journals. The first, *The German Quarterly,* is devoted chiefly to literary pursuits, but does include reviews of tests and other items of interest to language teachers. The second, *Die Unterricht-spraxis,* is devoted primarily to articles about the teaching of the German language. The AATG sponsors a teacher placement bureau, competitive exams for students, supplemental publications, annual meetings and a teacher information and service center which is co-sponsored by the National Carl Schurz Association.

### American Association of Teachers of Italian*
D. Frank, 1742 Tomlinson Ave., Bronx, N.Y. 10461

### American Association of Teachers of Slavic and Eastern European Languages
Joe Malik, Jr., Modern Languages 340, University of Arizona, Tucson, Ariz. 85721

AATSEEL publishes *Slavic and East European Journal* and *AATSEEL's Newsletter.* It also sponsors an honor society for students, state chapters, and supplemental publications.

### American Association of Teachers of Spanish and Portuguese
Richard Klein, Executive Secretary, College of the Holy Cross, Worcester, Ma. 01610

The AATSP publishes *Hispania,* which includes features of interest to all Spanish teachers. In addition, the AATSP sponsors flights to Spain, an honor society, competitive exams for students, annual meetings, state chapters, traveling displays of realia, a placement bureau, and other services.

*American Classical League*
> Department of Classics, Miami University, Oxford, O. 45056.
>
> The ACL maintains a full program for Latin teachers which includes its own publication, *Classical Outlook,* and those of several regional groups.

*American Council of Teachers of Uncommonly Taught Asian Languages (ACTU-AL)\**
> Soenjono Darjowidjojo, Department of Indo-Pacific Languages, University of Hawaii, Honolulu, Ha. 96822

*American Council on the Teaching of Foreign Languages (ACTFL)*
> C. Edward Scebold, 62 Fifth Avenue, New York, N.Y. 10011
>
> Originally under the fiscal supervision of the Modern Language Association and now beginning to incorporate itself as an independent group, ACTFL was founded to serve teachers of all languages. It publishes *Foreign Language Annals* to disseminate research reports and circulate news of the profession. That journal has merged with the former *Accent on ACTFL* which features articles on classroom teaching techniques. ACTFL sponsors an annual information and materials center. The *ACTFL Review of Foreign Language Education* reviews each year's progress in language teaching in a thematically oriented volume which is a rich source of information about current projects in language teaching. Student memberships in ACTFL (and in other major groups) are available. Methods students should be encouraged to join ACTFL and the language-oriented association of their choice, along with appropriate regional, state and local branches.

*Association of Teachers of Japanese\**
> Sumako Kimizuka, Department of Asian Studies, University of Southern California, University Park, Los Angeles, Cal. 90007

*Chinese Language Teachers Association\**
> John De Francis, University of Hawaii, Honolulu, Ha. 96822

*Modern Greek Studies Association\**
> Anne Farmakides, McGill University, Montreal 2, P.Q., Canada

*Modern Language Association*
> 62 Fifth Avenue, New York, N.Y. 10011
>
> The MLA publishes *PMLA* which includes an annual bibliography that has, over the years, become an indispensable tool for literary critics and scholars. The organization's most important role for the language specialist is that of a national center for information on language study. ACTFL is an organizational offshoot of the MLA, but the MLA remains of interest to language teachers because of its work, until 1974, as caretaker of MLA-ERIC, sponsor of numerous supplemental publications about language teaching, parent organization of the Association of Departments of Foreign Languages, and over-all public spokesman and representative of the language teaching profession.

*National Association of Language Laboratory Directors*

Dale Lally, Treasurer, University of Louisville, Department of Modern Languages, Louisville, Ky. 40208.

As the publisher of the *NALLD Journal,* this group provides information of interest to all who use audiovisual equipment of any kind to teach foreign languages. Journal articles provide reports on recent research, along with such unique information as pre-recorded tape exchanges, etc.

*Teachers of English to Speakers of Other Languages*

James E. Alatis, Georgetown University, Washington, D.C. 20007.

TESOL distributes *The TESOL Quarterly, The TESOL Newsletter,* and a number of supplemental publications. The *Quarterly* often provides information that is useful to teachers of all second languages. TESOL sponsors an annual meeting and several regional activities.

Several of the above groups have national, regional, state, and local chapters. Still other groups operate only regionally. All such groups are listed at least once per year either in the pages of *Foreign Language Annals* or in the chapter lists released by other professional journals.

Travel to national meetings is often difficult. Regional, state, and local meetings are the only opportunities many teachers have to meet their colleagues. But a new idea brought home from even a local meeting often makes the difference between the kind of job satisfaction that leads to success and the kind of ennui that leads to failure. It is part of our duty as methods teachers to encourage our students to join regional, state, and local associations as well as the national groups. Membership blanks secured from association offices or photocopied from journals should be distributed in class. Officials of state groups should be invited to address students, and students should be brought into contact with professionally active classroom teachers. Needless to say, all this assumes that the methods teacher must devote a certain proportion of his own time to such organizations. The resultant success of even a few of our graduates becomes more than sufficient payment for that time.

## Professional journals and aids

The value of membership in professional groups is enhanced by a continued effort to keep up-to-date by reading. The following are some of the journals and aids that methods students should be familiar with.

*ACTFL Annual Review of Foreign Language Education*

(formerly titled *Britannica Review of Foreign Language Education*), Skokie, Ill.: National Textbook Co. Issued annually, late in the year.

Each year the American Council on the Teaching of Foreign Languages (ACTFL) sponsors a review of the year's progress in foreign language education. Each volume is organized in accordance with a particular theme—individualized instruction, for an example. The chapters deal with varying aspects of the theme.

*American Foreign Language Teacher*
Post Office Box 07300, Detroit, Mich. 48207

*AFLT,* until the summer, 1974 issue, was published four times a year. Each issue included a poster for classroom display and some visuals which could be duplicated and used in class to stimulate interest and conversation. Articles tended to be specific and procedural in nature. Many of the articles were written by classroom teachers.

*Audio-Visual Language Journal*
D. Coleman, 33 The Larun Beat, Yarm. on Tries, North Yorkshire, England

While the articles in this British journal are not vastly different from those in many American ones, the books mentioned in the footnotes, advertisements, and reviews often are. Thus, *AVLJ* provides a convenient way to become aware of a significant number of British materials about foreign language teaching that may not be readily available here, but can be imported with relative ease.

*Canadian Modern Language Review*
P. K. Hambly, 34 Butternut Street, Toronto, Ont. M4KIT7, Canada

Topics covered in the quarterly issues of *CMLR* include suggestions for the adaptation of materials to meet local needs, innovations, methodological suggestions, and new types of tests. The focus of the journal is on classroom practice, rather than on theoretical considerations.

*Current Index to Journals in Education (CIJE)*

*CIJE* indexes most journals of interest to language teachers, making it possible to find articles on language teaching with relative ease. Unlike the *Education Index* which also indexes journals in education, *CIJE* indexes articles by authors. Large libraries are equipped to search the CIJE file by computer for a service fee.

*Die Unterrichtspraxis*

*Die Unterrichtspraxis* is one of two journals published by the American Association of Teachers of German. It deals with topics in foreign language education. Since many articles are in English, it can prove valuable to those intending to teach languages other than German.

*Education Digest*
Prakken Publications, P.O. Box 623, 416 Longshore Drive, Ann Arbor, Mich. 48107

Each month this publication presents condensations of articles in recent issues of all major journals and magazines in the field of education. Book reviews and listings of pamphlets are also included along with a section on news of governmental activities in education.

### Educational Resource Information Center (ERIC)

Most larger libraries are equipped with this collection of educational documents in microfiche form. Each plastic card in the collection accommodates at least 60 pages of printed material which can be magnified on a reading machine or transferred to a standard size paper format with a reader-printer. The collection grows at the rate of 1000 documents per month and is indexed by the governmental publication, *Research in Education*. Generally, at least one university library in each state is equipped to search the ERIC index by computer for a service fee. Foreign language documents are added to the collection by the MLA-ERIC Clearinghouse. Among the documents included are teacher-made materials, speeches, research reports, bibliographies, and curriculum guides. No methods student should leave school unaware of this significant resource. Additional information appears in each issue of *Foreign Language Annals*.

### French Review

*French Review* is the journal of the American Association of Teachers of French (AATF). It features literary articles along with ones on French culture, the teaching of French, and reviews of texts and other publications.

### Foreign Language Annals

*FLA*, incorporating *Accent on ACTFL,* is a quarterly journal published by The American Council on the Teaching of Foreign Languages (ACTFL). It features research in foreign language education, regular reports on the services of the MLA-ERIC Clearinghouse, and information such as directories and enrollment reports. The "ACTFL Annual Bibliography of Books and Articles on Foreign Language Pedagogy" in each May issue of *FLA* is one of the most current and comprehensive research tools available to the profession.

### German Quarterly

*GQ* is published by the American Association of Teachers of German. Articles are primarily literary in nature because education-oriented materials are published in *Die Unterrichtspraxis*. Methods students, however, will find the reviews and other smaller features of *GQ* quite useful.

### Hispania

*Hispania* is the journal of The American Association of Teachers of Spanish and Portuguese. Much of this journal deals with literary themes. Other interests covered include FLES, Spanish teaching, linguistic analyses, book and film reviews, and cultural information in the form of abstracted news reports.

### The Instructor

Dansville, N.Y. 14437

The intended audience of this publication is the elementary school classroom teacher. Nevertheless, it proves a rich source for the methods student in search of first language teaching ideas that can be adapted for use in second language classrooms.

### International Review of Applied Linguistics
Julius Groos Verlag, P.O. Box 629, 6900 Heidelberg, Germany

*IRAL* is one of the world's best known journals of experimental applications of linguistic theory to language teaching practice. Of its many features, the undergraduate methods student will most likely attach the greatest value to the detailed analyses presented in the reviews and the wide range of sources it brings together. Students of French and German will also appreciate the material on language pedagogy in their second languages.

### Language and Language Behavior Abstracts
Suite 256, City Center Bldg., 220 E. Huron St., Ann Arbor, Mich. 48108

From 1967 to 1975, *LLBA* reviewed and abstracted articles from more than 1000 journals representing the work of scholars in approximately twenty-five language-related disciplines from nearly all the countries of the world. Both theoretical studies and articles oriented toward classroom practice were included. The publishers of *Sociological Abstracts* will release subsequent volumes of *LLBA*.

### Language Learning
2001 N. University Boulevard, University of Michigan, Ann Arbor, Mich. 48104

Theoretical and practical aspects of language acquisition and second language pedagogy are the general themes of this semi-annual publication. Reviews and analytical bibliographies are also featured.

### Language Teaching and Linguistics: Abstracts
Cambridge University Press (American Branch), 32 East 57th Street, New York, N.Y. 10022

*LTLA* abstracts cover approximately 200 magazines and journals in the field of language teaching from around the world. Brief digests in English are given for each article selected.

### Learning: The Magazine for Creative Teaching
1255 Portland Place, Boulder, Col. 80302

*Learning,* like *The Instructor,* is intended for the elementary school classroom teacher. It does, however, contain an occasional item directed to second language teachers specifically. Even when it does not, many of the ideas presented are adaptable for use in second language classrooms.

### The Modern Language Journal
Wallace G. Klein, 13149 Cannes Drive, St. Louis, Mo. 63141

The *MLJ* has been publishing articles on methods and pedagogical research in language teaching for approximately 60 years. Published by The National Federation of Modern Language Teachers' Associations, it also includes professional news and notes and book reviews. The *MLJ* is an invaluable resource for teachers and students alike. The journal's business manager will make arrangements for a special two-issue subscription for methods students.

### National Society for the Study of Education Yearbook

Available from University of Chicago Press, Chicago, Ill. 60637

Two volumes of the *NSSE Yearbook* are released each year. They deal with different areas of interest in education and are comprehensive in nature. Typically, the topics are subjects that apply to teachers of all disciplines (programmed instruction, for example).

### Reports of the Working Committees of the Northeast Conference

Northeast Conference, P.O. Box 623, Middlebury, Vt. 05753

Each year the Northeast Conference on the Teaching of Foreign Languages meets to discuss the annual reports of its working committees. Each year's reports center around a particular theme and are invariably useful as sources of current information.

### Slavic and East European Journal

*SEEJ* is the journal of the American Association of Teachers of Slavic and Eastern European languages. It treats literary topics primarily, but features reviews and other items of interest to language teachers as well.

### Spanish Today

P.O. Box 1269, Homestead, Fla. 33030

*Spanish Today* is a magazine of practical ideas and cultural features for high school Spanish teachers. Although the quality is not as even as that of some other publications, no issue is without something useful.

### TESOL Quarterly

*TESOL Quarterly* is the journal of Teachers of English to Speakers of Other Languages. Articles are usually pedagogical in nature and are often quite practical, in addition to being easily adaptable to other languages.

### Other aids to language teachers

Goldsmith's Music Shop, Inc.
301 E. Shore Road
Great Neck, Long Island, N.Y. 11023

Goldsmith's publishes separate catalogs for French, German, and Spanish.

National Textbook Co.
8259 Niles Center Road
Skokie, Ill. 60076

National Textbook will supply methods students with a 64-page catalog of supplementary materials. These include materials for cultural analyses, reading, and language club projects.

Newbury House Publishers, Inc.
68 Middle Road
Rowley, Mass. 01969

Newbury House publishes strictly in the area of language teaching, language science, and language learning. A catalog or listings are available on request.

Scholastic Publications
902 Sylvan Avenue
Englewood Cliffs, N.J. 07632

Scholastic publishes 10 classroom magazines for teaching reading skills in French, German, and Spanish. Samples for methods students are available.

J. Weston Walsh
Portland, Maine 04104

Walsh's publication list includes books on language games and club projects.

Wible Language Institute
24 South Eighth Street
Allentown, Pa. 18105

Wible supplies slide sets, visuals, and other language teaching aids. A 101-page catalog is available for teaching of French, German, and Spanish.

Xerox Education Publications
Education Center
Columbus, O. 43216

Xerox publishes magazines in Spanish and French for three levels of instruction. Records accompany the magazines to aid the teaching of reading skills. The company supplies copies of the magazines in quantities for methods classes.

## CONCLUSION

This chapter has presented resources to investigate historical and theoretical considerations, classroom practice, and professional outreach. In an era known as that of "the knowledge explosion," professional preparation must extend beyond the walls of the methods classroom. The methods teacher bears an obligation to model effective professional growth for his students as he encourages them to extend their professional preparation. The sources of information presented here are intended to stimulate and enhance that growth. A list of reference works used in this chapter is to be found at the end of the book.

## CHAPTER 1 Listening, Reading and the Methods Course

Allen, Dwight and Kevin Ryan, 1969. *Microteaching.* Reading (Mass.): Addison-Wesley.

Allen, Edward David and Rebecca M. Valette, 1972. *Modern Language Classroom Techniques.* New York: Harcourt Brace Jovanovich.

Asher, James, 1969. "The Total Physical Response Approach to Second Language Learning." *Modern Language Journal 53*: 3-17.

Birkmaier, Emma and William Jack, 1967. *Acquiring Foreign Language Reading Skills.* St. Paul: Minnesota State Department of Education. (ERIC Document Reproduction Service: ED 014 930).

Busse, Bonnie B., 1972. "Innovation in the Professional Preparation of Foreign Language Teachers." *The Bulletin of the Illinois Foreign Language Teachers Association 4*: 20-27.

Christiansen, Heinz C., 1972. "Eye-to-Eye Teaching: An Approach to Reading Courses." *Foreign Language Annals 6*: 447-450.

Culhane, Joseph W., 1970. "CLOZE Procedures and Comprehension." *The Reading Teacher 23*: 410-413.

Elkins, Robert J., Theodore B. Kalivoda and Genelle Morain, 1972. "Teaching Culture through the Audio-Motor Unit." *Foreign Language Annals 6*: 61-67.

Garfinkel, Alan, 1972. "The Enrichment-Oriented Radio Program: A Medium for Building Listening Comprehension Skills." *Hispania 55*: 310-312.

Goodman, Kenneth S., 1971. "Psycholinguistic Universals in the Reading Process," in (Paul Pimsleur and Terence Quinn, eds.) *The Psychology of Second Language Learning* (papers presented at the Second International Congress of Applied Linguistics, Cambridge, 8-12 September 1969). Cambridge: Cambridge University Press, pp. 135-142.

Grittner, Frank, 1969. *Teaching Foreign Languages.* New York: Harper & Row.

Huberman, Gisela and Vadim Medish, 1974. "A Multi-Channel Approach to Language Teaching." *Foreign Language Annals 7*: 674-680.

Instructional Objectives Exchange, 1970. (P.O. Box 24095, Los Angeles). *Spanish Grades 7-12.* USOE HEW, UCLA.

# Bibliography

Jakobovits, Leon A., 1968 (1969). "Physiology and Psychology of Second Language Learning," in (Emma M. Birkmaier, ed.) *Britannica Review of Foreign Language Education,* Volume 1. Chicago: Encyclopedia Britannica, Inc., pp. 181-227.

Jarvis, Gilbert A., 1970. "Strategies of Instruction for Listening and Reading," in (Dale L. Lange, ed.) *Britannica Review of Foreign Language Education,* Volume 2. Chicago: Encylopedia Britannica Inc., pp. 79-111.

———, 1973. "Comments on 'Uses of Reading.'" *Modern Language Journal 57*: 396-399.

Kalivoda, Theodore B., Genelle Morain and Robert J. Elkins, 1971. "The Audio-Motor Unit: A Listening Comprehension Strategy that Works." *Foreign Language Annals 4*: 392-400.

Lohnes, Walter, 1967. "Some New Approaches on How to Teach Reading," in (Emma Birkmaier and William Jack) *Acquiring Foreign Language Reading Skills.* St. Paul: Minnesota State Department of Education, 1967, pp. 28-38. (ERIC Document Reproduction Service: ED 014 930)

Michel, Joseph (ed.), 1967. *Foreign Language Teaching.* New York: Macmillan.

Mueller, Theodore, 1974. "Another Look at How to Teach Listening and Reading Comprehension." *Modern Language Journal 58*: 19-23.

Parent, P. Paul and Simon Belasco, 1970. "Parallel Column Bilingual Reading Material as a Pedagogical Device: An Experimental Evaluation." *Modern Language Journal 54*: 493-504.

Phillips, June K., 1975. "Second Language Reading: Teaching Decoding Skills." *Foreign Language Annals 8*: 227-232.

Politzer, Robert L., 1966. *Practice-Centered Teacher Training: French.* Philadelphia: Center for Curriculum Development.

Politzer, Robert L. and Diana E. Bartley, 1967. *Practice-Centered Teacher Training: Spanish.* Philadelphia: Center for Curriculum Development.

Rivers, Wilga, 1968. *Teaching Foreign Language Skills.* Chicago: University of Chicago Press.

———, 1972. "Linguistic and Psychological Factors in Speech Perception and Their Implications for Teaching Materials," *Speaking in Many Tongues.* Rowley (Mass.): Newbury House, pp. 94-107.

Rivers, Wilga et al., 1975a. *A Practical Guide to the Teaching of French.* New York: Oxford University Press.

———, 1975b. *A Practical Guide to the Teaching of German.* New York: Oxford University Press.

Santoni, Georges V., 1972. "Methods of Teaching Literature." *Foreign Language Annals 5*: 432-441.

Scherer, G. A. C. et al., 1963. "Reading for Meaning," in (W. F. Bottiglia, ed.) *Language Learning: The Intermediate Phase. Reports of the Working Committee, 1963 Northeast Conference on the Teaching of Foreign Languages.* New York: Northeast Conference, pp. 22-60. (Available from the Northeast Conference, Middlebury College, Middlebury, Vt.)

Seelye, H. Ned and J. Laurance Day, 1971. "Penetrating the Mass Media: A Unit to Develop Skill in Reading Spanish Newspaper Headlines." *Foreign Language Annals 5*: 69-81.

Stack, Edward M., 1966. *The Language Laboratory and Modern Language Teaching.* New York: Oxford University Press.

Starr, Wilmarth H. et al. (eds.), 1960. *Modern Foreign Languages and the Academically Talented Student.* Washington: National Education Association.

Steiner, Florence, 1975. *Performing with Objectives.* Rowley (Mass.): Newbury House.

Strang, Ruth, 1969. *Diagnostic Teaching of Reading.* New York: McGraw-Hill.

Stubbs, Joseph B. and G. Richard Tucker, 1974. "The CLOZE Test as a Measure of English Proficiency." *Modern Language Journal 58*: 239-241.

Twadell, Freeman, 1973. "Uses of Reading." *Modern Language Journal 57*: 393-396.

Valette, Rebecca M., 1969. *Directions in Foreign Language Testing.* New York: Modern Language Association (MLA-ACTFL Materials Center).

———, 1967. *Modern Language Testing.* New York: Harcourt Brace Jovanovich.

Valette, Rebecca M. and Renée Disick, 1972. *Modern Language Performance Objectives and Individualization.* New York: Harcourt Brace Jovanovich.

Wardhaugh, Ronald, 1974. *Topics in Applied Linguistics.* Rowley (Mass.): Newbury House.

## CHAPTER 2 Speaking, Writing and the Methods Course

Asher, James J., 1969. "The Total Physical Response Approach to Second Language Learning." *Modern Language Journal 53*: 3-17.

Ausubel, D. P., 1964. "Adults vs. Children in Second Language Learning: Psychological Considerations." *Modern Language Journal 48*: 420-424.

Belyayev, B. V., 1964. *The Psychology of Teaching Foreign Languages.* New York: Pergamon Press.

Damoiseau, Robert, 1969. "La Classe de Conversation." *Le Français dans le Monde 65*: 58-62.

Flaxman, S. L. (ed.), 1961. "Modern Language Teaching in School and College." *Northeast Conference on the Teaching of Foreign Languages: Reports of the Working Committees.* New York: Northeast Conference. (Available from the Northeast Conference, Middlebury College, Middlebury, Vt.)

Hawkins, Lee E., 1972. "Extra-School Factors that Influence Language Learning." *The ACTFL Review of Foreign Language Education,* Vol. 4. Skokie (Ill.): National Textbook Company.

Joiner, Elizabeth G., 1974. "Keep Them Guessing." *American Foreign Language Teacher 4*, ii: 16-18.

Lenneberg, Eric H. (ed.), 1964. *New Directions in the Study of Language.* Cambridge (Mass.): M.I.T. Press.

Longstreet, Wilma S., n.d. "Ethnic Characteristics: A Plan of Action." Unpublished manuscript.

Lowry, William H. and Robert R. Reilly, 1970. "Life Problems and Interests of Adolescents." *The Clearing House 45*: 164-168.

McKay, Llewelyn R., 1960. "Some Pitfalls in Teaching Foreign Languages." *School and Society, 88* (Nov.): 419-420.

Parker, Don H., 1970. "When Should I Individualize Instruction?" in (Virgil M. Howes, ed.) *Individualization of Instruction: A Teaching Strategy.* New York: Macmillan.

Paulston, Christina Bratt, 1972. "Teaching Writing in the ESOL Classroom: Techniques of Controlled Composition." *TESOL Quarterly 6*, i: 33-59.

Rivers, Wilga M., 1968. *Teaching Foreign-Language Skills.* Chicago: University of Chicago Press. p. 299.

———, 1972. *Speaking in Many Tongues.* Rowley (Mass.): Newbury House.

Savignon, Sandra J., 1972. "Teaching for Communicative Competence: A Research Report." *The Audio-Visual Language Journal 10*: 153-162.

Stack, Edward M., 1973. *The Language Laboratory and Modern Language Teaching,* 3d ed. New York: Oxford University Press.

Troyanovich, John, 1974. "How Defensible is Writing as an Objective in Short-Term Foreign Language Experiences?" *Foreign Language Annals 7* (May): 435-442.

Valette, Rebecca M., 1967. *Modern Language Testing: A Handbook.* New York: Harcourt Brace Jovanovich.

## CHAPTER 3 — OTHER REFERENCES ON FOREIGN CULTURE STUDY
The Cultural Component of the Methods Course

### Folklore in the foreign language classroom

Campa, Arthur L., 1969. *Teaching Hispanic Culture Through Folklore.* MLA/ERIC Focus Report 2. New York: Modern Language Association Materials Center.

Morain, Genelle, 1969. *French Culture: The Folklore Facet.* MLA/ERIC Focus Report 9. New York: Modern Language Association Materials Center.

Weiss, Gerhard H., 1969. *Folktale and Folklore—Useful Cultural Tools for Teachers of German.* MLA/ERIC Focus Report 6. New York: Modern Language Association Materials Center.

### Kinesics

Birdwhistell, Ray L., 1970. *Kinesics and Context: Essays on Body Motion Communication.* Philadelphia: University of Pennsylvania Press.

Brault, Gerald J., 1963. "Kinesics and the Classroom: Some Typical French Gestures." *The French Review 36.*

Green, Jerald R., 1971. "A Focus Report: Kinesics in the Foreign Language Classroom." *Foreign Language Annals 5*: 62-68.

———, 1969. *A Gesture Inventory for the Teaching of Spanish.* Philadelphia: Chilton Books.

### Cultural materials for specific languages

*French Culture*

Bouraoui, H. A., 1971. *Créaculture I* and *Créaculture II.* Philadelphia: Center for Curriculum Development.

Jay, Charles, and Pat Castle (eds.), 1971. *French Language Education: The Teaching of Culture in the Classroom.* Springfield (Ill.): State Department of Public Instruction.

Nostrand, Howard L., n.d. *Background Data for the Teaching of French:* Final Report of Project OE-6-14-005. Part A: *La Culture et la société françaises au XXe siècle,* 2 vols.; Part B: *Exemples littéraires*; Part C: *Contemporary culture and society of the United States.* Seattle: Department of Romance Languages and Literature, University of Washington.

Rey, Jean-Noël, and Georges Santoni, 1975. *Quand Les Français Parlent.* Rowley (Mass.): Newbury House.

Wylie, Laurence and Armand Begue, 1970. *Les Français.* Englewood Cliffs (N.J.): Prentice-Hall.

*German Culture*

Schalk, Adolph et al., 1968. *These Strange German Ways,* 6th edition. Hamburg: Atlantik-Brücke.

Smith, Duncan (Special Editor), 1971. "Focus on German Culture and Civilization." *Die Unterrichtspraxis 4,* no. 1: 30-91.

Weiss, Gerhard and Charlotte Anderson, 1970. *Begegnung mit Deutschland.* New York: Dodd, Mead.

## Spanish Culture

Seelye, H. Ned (ed.), 1968. *A Handbook on Latin America for Teachers: Methodology and Annotated Bibliography*. Springfield (Ill.): Office of Public Instruction.

———, 1970. *Perspectives for Teachers of Latin American Culture*. Springfield (Ill.): State Department of Public Instruction, Division of Instruction.

Seelye, H. Ned and J. Laurence Day, 1971. "Penetrating the Mass Media: A Unit to Develop Skill in Reading Spanish Newspaper Headlines." *Foreign Language Annals 5*: 69-81.

## Overview of the teaching of culture in the foreign language classroom

Altman, Howard B. and Victor E. Hanzeli (eds.), 1974. *Essays on the Teaching of Culture*: A Festschrift to Honor Howard Lee Nostrand. Detroit: Advancement Press of America.

Lafayette Robert C. et al. (eds.), 1975. *The Culture Revolution in Foreign Language Teaching*. Skokie (Ill.): National Textbook Co.

Morain, Genelle, 1970 (1971). "Cultural Pluralism," in (Dale Lange, ed.) *Britannica Review of Foreign Language Education, Volume 3*. Chicago: Encyclopaedia Britannica, Inc. pp. 59-95.

Nostrand, Howard L., 1974. "Empathy for a second culture: Motivations and techniques," in (Gilbert A. Jarvis, ed.) *Responding to New Realities: The ACTFL Review of Foreign Language Education, Volume 5*. Skokie (Ill.): National Textbook Co. pp. 263-327.

Seelye, H. Ned, 1968 (1969). "Analysis and Teaching of the Cross-Cultural Context," in (Emma Birkmaier, ed.) *Britannica Review of Foreign Language Education*, Volume 1. Chicago: Encyclopaedia Britannica, Inc. pp. 59-95.

———, 1974. *Teaching Culture: Strategies for Foreign Language Educators*. Skokie (Ill.): National Textbook Co.

## CHAPTER 4   Training Teachers for the Affective Dimension of the Curriculum

### On affective education

Alschuler, Alfred S., Diane Tabor, and James McIntyre, 1971. *Teaching Achievement Motivation*. Middletown (Conn.): Education Ventures.

Bessel, Harold, and Uvaldo Palomares, 1973. *Methods in Human Development Theory Manual*. San Diego (Cal.): Human Development Training Institute.

Brown, George Isaac, 1971. *Human Teaching for Human Learning: An Introduction to Confluent Education*. New York: Viking Press.

Harmin, Merrill, Howard Kirschenbaum, and Sidney B. Simon, 1973. *Clarifying Values Through Subject Matter*. Minneapolis (Minn.): Winston Press.

Hawley, Robert C., 1975. *Value Exploration Through Role Playing*. New York: Hart Publishing Company.

Hawley, Robert C., and Isabel L. Hawley, 1975. *Human Values in the Classroom*. New York: Hart Publishing Company.

Hawley, Robert C., Sidney B. Simon and David D. Britton, 1973. *Composition for Personal Growth*. New York: Hart Publishing Company.

Hebeisen, Ardyth, 1973. *PEER Program for Youth*. Minneapolis (Minn.): Augsburg Press.

Howe, Leland W., and Mary Martha Howe, 1975. *Personalizing Education: Values Clarification and Beyond*. New York: Hart Publishing Company.

James, Muriel, and Dorothy Jongeward, 1971. *Born to Win: Transactional Analysis with Gestalt Experiments*. Reading (Mass.): Addison-Wesley.

Johnson, David W., 1972. *Reading Out. Interpersonal Effectiveness and Self-Actualization.* Englewood Cliffs (N.J.): Prentice-Hall.

Krupar, Karen R., 1973. *Communication Games.* New York: Free Press.

Lyon, Harold C., Jr., 1971. *Learning to Feel—Feeling to Learn.* Columbus (Ohio): Charles E. Merrill.

Maslow, Abraham, 1971. "Goals and Implications of Humanistic Education," in *The Farther Reaches of Human Nature.* New York: Viking Press.

———, 1954 (1970). *Motivation and Personality.* New York: Harper & Row.

Perls, Frederick S., 1971. *Gestalt Therapy Verbatim.* New York: Bantam Press.

Raths, Louis E., Merrill Harmin, and Sidney B. Simon, 1966. *Values and Teaching: Working with Values in the Classroom.* Columbus (Ohio): Charles E. Merrill.

Rogers, Carl R., 1969. *Freedom to Learn.* Columbus (Ohio): Charles E. Merrill.

Simon, Sidney B., Leland W. Howe, and Howard Kirschenbaum, 1972. *Values Clarification: A Handbook of Practical Strategies for Teachers and Students.* New York: Hart Publishing Company.

Simon, Sidney B., and Howard Kirschenbaum (eds.), 1973. *Readings in Values Clarification.* Minneapolis (Minn.): Winston Press.

Weinstein, Gerald, and Mario Fantini, 1970. *Toward Humanistic Education: A Curriculum of Affect.* New York: Praeger.

## On affective education and foreign language teaching

Born, Warren C. (ed.), 1974. *Toward Student-Centered Foreign Language Programs.* Reports of the Working Committees of the Northeast Conference on the Teaching of Foreign Languages. New York: Modern Language Association Materials Center. pp. 87-95.

Christensen, Clay Benjamin, 1975. "Affective Learning Activities (ALA)," *Foreign Language Annals 8*: 211-219.

Disick, Renée S., 1975. *Individualizing Language Instruction: Strategies and Methods.* New York: Harcourt Brace Jovanovich.

Disick, Renée S., and Laura Barbanel, 1974. "Affective Education and Foreign Learning," in (Gilbert A. Jarvis, ed.) *The Challenge of Communication.* ACTFL Review of Foreign Language Education, Volume 6. Skokie (Ill.): National Textbook Company.

Gabriel, Toni, 1973. "Mind Expanding." *American Foreign Language Teacher 4*, 1: 25-26.

Jarvis, Gilbert A., 1975. "We Think We Are *Evening in Paris,* But We're Really *Chanel." Foreign Language Annals 8*, 2: 104-110.

Love, F. William D., and Lucille J. Honig, 1973. *Options and Perspectives: A Sourcebook of Innovative Foreign Language Programs in Action, K-12.* New York: Modern Language Association of America. pp. 65-77, 215-224, and 243-252.

Morel, Stefano, 1974. *Human Dynamics in Italian.* Upper Jay (N.Y.): Adirondack Mountain Humanistic Education Center. Also available in Spanish, French, and German.

Stoller, Phyllis S., and Joanne Tuskes Lock, 1974. *Real Communication in French.* Upper Jay (N.Y.): Adirondack Mountain Humanistic Education Center.

Wilson, Virginia, and Beverly Wattenmaker, 1973a. *Real Communication in Foreign Language and Real Communication in Spanish.* Upper Jay (N.Y.): Adirondack Mountain Humanistic Education Center.

———, 1973b. "Teaching Foreign Language Without Failure," in (Herman F. Bostick and Gail Hutchinson, eds.) *Dimension: Languages '72.* Proceedings of the 1972 Joint Annual Meeting of ACTFL and SCOLT. New York: American Council on the Teaching of Foreign Languages.

Wolfe, David E., 1973. "Toward a Confluent Approach." *Modern Language Journal 57*: 113-119.

Wolfe, David E., and Leland W. Howe, 1973. "Personalizing Foreign Language Instruction." *Foreign Language Annals 7*: 81-90.

Wolfe, David E., Leland W. Howe, and Marianne Keating, 1973. "Clarifying Values Through Foreign Language Study." *Hispania 56*: 404-406.

# CHAPTER 5 Individualized Instruction and the Foreign Language Methods Course

Allen, Edward D., 1971. "The Foreign Language Teacher as a Learner in the Seventies." *Modern Language Journal 55*: 203-207.

Altman, Howard B., 1971. "Some Practical Aspects of Individualized Foreign Language Instruction," in (George W. Wilkins, Jr., ed.) *Dimension: Languages 71. Proceedings of the Seventh Southern Conference on Language Teaching.* New York: MLA–ACTFL Materials Center.

———, 1972a. "Training the Foreign Language Teacher for Individualization." *NALLD Journal 6*, iv: 7-11.

Altman, Howard B. (ed.), 1972b. *Individualizing the Foreign Language Classroom: Perspectives for Teachers.* Rowley (Mass.): Newbury House.

Altman, Howard B., and Robert L. Politzer (eds.), 1971. *Individualizing Foreign Language Instruction: Proceedings of the Stanford Conference.* Rowley (Mass.): Newbury House.

Arendt, Jermaine D., 1970. "Media in Foreign Language Teaching," in (Dale L. Lange, ed.) *Britannica Review of Foreign Language Education,* Vol. 2. Chicago: Encyclopedia Britannica, Inc.

———, 1971. "The Function and Techniques of Group Work in an Individualized Program," in (Howard B. Altman and Robert L. Politzer, eds.) *Individualizing Foreign Language Instruction: Proceedings of the Stanford Conference.* Rowley (Mass.): Newbury House.

Berwald, Jean-Pierre, 1974. "Supervising Student Teachers in Individualized Foreign Language Classes." *Modern Language Journal 58*: 91-95.

Bockman, John F., 1971. "The Process of Contracting," in (Howard B. Altman and Robert L. Politzer, eds.) *Individualizing Foreign Language Instruction: Proceedings of the Stanford Conference.* Rowley (Mass.): Newbury House.

Bockman, John F., and Ronald Gougher (eds.), 1970-1975. "Individualized Instruction." This column appears in each recent issue of *Foreign Language Annals* beginning with Vol. 4, No. 4.

Braswell, David M., 1972. "Individualizing the Junior High School FL Curriculum," in (Howard B. Altman, ed.) *Individualizing the Foreign Language Classroom: Perspectives for Teachers.* Rowley (Mass.): Newbury House.

Buchanan, M. Marcia, 1971. "Preparing Teachers to be Persons." *Phi Delta Kappan 52*, 10 (June): 614-617.

Bull, William E. et al., 1971. *Spanish for Communication.* Boston: Houghton Mifflin.

Clark, Arvel B., 1971. "Planning for Individualizing Instruction: An Administrator's Perspective," in (Howard B. Altman and Robert L. Politzer, eds.) *Individualizing Foreign Language Instruction: Proceedings of the Stanford Conference.* Rowley (Mass.): Newbury House.

Dell, Helen Davis, 1972. *Individualizing Instruction: Materials and Classroom Procedures.* Chicago: Science Research Associates, Inc.

Dellaccio, Carl et al., 1971. "Administrative Issues in Individualization of Foreign Language Instruction" and "Reports and Recommendations of the Committee," in (Howard B. Altman and Robert L. Politzer, eds.) *Individualizing Foreign Language Instruction: Proceedings of the Stanford Conference.* Rowley (Mass.): Newbury House.

Disick, Renée S., 1972. "Developing Positive Attitudes in Intermediate Foreign Language Classes." *Modern Language Journal 56*: 417-420.

Edgerton, Mills F., Jr. (ed.), 1969. *Sight and Sound: The Sensible and Sensitive Use of Audio-Visual Aids. Northeast Conference on the Teaching of Foreign Languages.* Middlebury (Vt.): The Northeast Conference, Middlebury College.

Flanders, Ned A., 1970. *Analyzing Teaching Behavior.* Reading (Mass.): Addison-Wesley.

Gardner, R. C., and W. E. Lambert, 1972. *Attitudes and Motivation in Second-Language Learning.* Rowley (Mass.): Newbury House.

Hanzeli, Victor E., and F. William Love, 1972. "From Individualized Instruction to Individualized Learning." *Foreign Language Annals 5*: 321-330.

Hocking, Elton, 1971. "The Role of 'Hardware' in Individualizing Foreign Language Instruction: Present and Potential," in (Howard B. Altman and Robert L. Politzer, eds.) *Individualizing Foreign Language Instruction: Proceedings of the Stanford Conference.* Rowley (Mass.): Newbury House.

Kapfer, Philip G., and Gardner Swenson, 1968. "Individualizing Instruction for Self-Paced Learning." *The Clearing House 42*: 405-410.

Logan, Gerald E., 1970. "Curricula for Individualized Instruction," in (Dale L. Lange, ed.) *Britannica Review of Foreign Language Education,* Vol. 2. Chicago: Encyclopedia Britannica, Inc.

———, 1971. "Problems in Testing, Grading, and Issuing Credits in an Individualized Foreign Language Program," in (Howard B. Altman and Robert L. Politzer, eds.) *Individualizing Foreign Language Instruction: Proceedings of the Stanford Conference.* Rowley (Mass.): Newbury House.

———, 1973. *Individualized Foreign Language Learning: An Organic Process.* Rowley (Mass.): Newbury House.

McKim, Lester W., 1972. "Planning for Individualization: A Necessary Look Before Leaping," in (Howard B. Altman, ed.) *Individualizing the Foreign Language Classroom: Perspectives for Teachers.* Rowley (Mass.): Newbury House.

Morrey, Robert A., 1972. "Individualization of Foreign Language Instruction Through Differentiated Staffing." *Modern Language Journal 56*: 483-488.

Moskowitz, Gertrude, 1968. "The Effects of Training Foreign Language Teachers in Interaction Analysis." *Foreign Language Annals 1*: 218-235.

———, 1970. "Interaction Analysis." *American Foreign Language Teacher 1,* i: 10-15.

———, 1972. "Interaction Analysis–A New Modern Language for Supervisors." *Foreign Language Annals 5*: 211-221.

Mueller, Theodore H., 1971. "The Development of Curricular Materials (including Programmed Materials) for Individualized Foreign Language Instruction," in (Howard B. Altman and Robert L. Politzer, eds.) *Individualizing Foreign Language Instruction: Proceedings of the Stanford Conference.* Rowley (Mass.): Newbury House.

Nelson, Robert J. et al., 1970. "Motivation in Foreign Language Learning," in (Joseph A. Tursi, ed.) *Foreign Languages and the 'New' Student. Northeast Conference on the Teaching of Foreign Languages.* Middlebury (Vt.): Northeast Conference, Middlebury College.

Papalia, Anthony, and Joseph Zampogna, 1972. "An Experimental Study on Teachers' Classroom Behaviors and Their Effect on FL Attrition." *Modern Language Journal 56*: 421-424.

Rivers, Wilga M., 1971. "Techniques for Developing Proficiency in the Spoken Language," in (Howard B. Altman and Robert L. Politzer, eds.) *Individualizing Foreign Language Instruction: Proceedings of the Stanford Conference.* Rowley (Mass.): Newbury House.

———, 1972. *Speaking in Many Tongues: Essays in Foreign Language Teaching.* Rowley (Mass.): Newbury House.

Rosenthal, Bianca, 1973. "Individualized Foreign Language Instruction: Developing a Learning Activity Package." *Modern Language Journal 57*: 195-199.

Ryberg, Donald C., and Marcia Hallock, 1972. "Development of Mini-Courses at Marshall-University High School: Individualization and Interest," in (Ronald L. Gougher, ed.) *Individualization in Foreign Languages: A Practical Guide.* Chicago: Rand McNally.

Smith, Alfred N., 1972. "How to Train Prospective Foreign Language Teachers in the Use of Individualized Instruction." *Foreign Language Annals 6*: 220-224.

Steiner, Florence, 1971. "Individualized Instruction." *Modern Language Journal 55*: 361-374.

Teetor, Will Robert, 1972. "Grading and Awarding Credit on a 'Humane' and Sensible Basis:

The Ithaca Experience," in (Ronald L. Gougher, ed.) *Individualization of Instruction in Foreign Languages: A Practical Guide*. Chicago: Rand McNally.

Valette, Rebecca M., and Renée S. Disick, 1972. *Modern Language Performance Objectives and Individualization: A Handbook*. New York: Harcourt Brace Jovanovich.

## CHAPTER 6 Training Graduate Assistants in Foreign Languages

Adams, M., 1969. "Classroom Method for University Language Teaching," *Babel 5*, ii: 18-22 (Australia).

Dalbor, John B., 1967. "A Realistic Look at the Training of College Foreign Language Teachers," *Modern Language Journal 51*: 209-214.

Dale, Edgar et al., 1971. *Techniques of Teaching Vocabulary*, Addison (Ill.): Field Educational Enterprises.

Delattre, P., 1966. "Principles of Language Instruction at the College Level," in (Sanford Newell, ed.) *Dimension: Languages 66*—Proceedings of SCOLT, Atlanta, Ga. (Feb. 1966). Available from Modern Language Association Materials Center, New York.

DeLorenzo, William E., 1971. "The Performance-Oriented Foreign Language Methods Course: A Partially Programmed Approach." Unpublished doctoral dissertation, The Ohio State University.

Hagiwara, Michio P., 1969. "Training and Supervision of College Foreign Language Teachers," *Foreign Language Annals 3*: 90-107.

———, 1970. "Training and Supervision of Graduate Teaching Assistants, Analysis of Programs, III, Implications for Departments," *ADFL: Bulletin of the Association of Departments of Foreign Languages 1*, iii: 44-50.

Hanzeli, Victor E., 1968. "Internship for Teaching Assistants," *Improving College and University Teaching 16*: 110-112.

Hester, Ralph M., 1970. "Direct Method Experiences at College and University Level" in (Ralph Hester, ed.) *Teaching a Living Language*. New York: Harper & Row.

Jian, Gerard, 1972. "Le Programme de Première Année à Berkley," *French Review 45*: 846-849.

Kalivoda, Theodore B., 1968. "The Methods Course and Lower Division Instruction." *Hispania 51*: 124-125.

Lenard, Yvonne, 1970. "Methods and Materials, Techniques and the Teacher," in (Ralph Hester, ed.) *Teaching a Living Language*, New York: Harper & Row.

MacAllister, Archibald T., 1964. "The Preparation of College Teachers of Modern Foreign Languages," *Publications of the Modern Language Association 79*: 29-43.

Meiden, Walter, 1970. "Training the Inexperienced Graduate Assistant for Language Teaching," *Modern Language Journal 54*: 168-174.

Modern Language Association Materials Center, 1961. *Foreign Language Teaching in College: A Set of Recommendations and Some Workpapers* (New York).

Mueller, Klaus A., 1972. "Aspects in Training and Supervising College Teachers of Foreign Languages," *Foreign Language Annals 5*: 236-239.

Øksenholt, Svein, 1963. "The Training of the Foreign Language Teaching Assistant," *Modern Language Journal 47*: 368-371.

Parnell, C., 1966. "Foreign Languages at College and University Level," in (Sanford Newell, ed.) *Dimension: Languages 66*—Proceedings of SCOLT. Atlanta, Ga. Southern Conference on Language Teaching. Available from Modern Language Association Materials Center.

Piedmont, Ferdinand, 1968. "Group Observation and the Training of Teaching Assistants," *Die Unterrichtspraxis I*, i: 82-86.

Roeming, Robert F., 1972. "Teaching of Foreign Languages: 4 Colleges and Universities," in

(Lee C. Deighton, ed.) *The Encyclopedia of Education,* Vol. 4. New York: Macmillan and the Free Press.

Stein, Jack M., 1961. "The Preparation of College and University Teachers," in (Seymour L. Flaxman, ed.) *Language Teaching in School and College.* New York: Northeast Conference. Available from MLA-ACTFL Materials Center.

## CHAPTER 7   Preparing Teachers for Non-English Home Language Learners

Andersson, Theodore and Mildred Boyer, 1970. *Bilingual Schooling in the United States, Volume II.* Washington: Superintendent of Documents. (This two-volume set, commissioned under USOE Title IV, contract number 4-7-062113-3072, by the Southwest Educational Development Laboratory, is for sale by the Superintendent of Documents, Government Printing Office at $6.00.)

Gaarder, Bruce et al., 1972. "Teaching Spanish in School and College to Native Speakers of Spanish." *Hispania 55*: 619-631.

Texas Education Agency, 1970. *Español para alumnos hispanohablantes.* Bethesda (Md.): ERIC Document Reproduction Service (ED 047 588).

## CHAPTER 8   A Methods Teacher's Guide to Information Sources

Allen, Dwight W., and Eli Seifman, 1971. *The Teacher's Handbook.* Glenview (Ill.): Scott, Foresman.

Allen, Edward David, and Rebecca M. Valette, 1972. *Modern Language Classroom Techniques: A Handbook,* New York: Harcourt Brace Jovanovich.

Altman, Howard B. (ed.), 1972. *Individualizing the Foreign Language Classroom: Perspectives for Teachers.* Rowley (Mass.): Newbury House.

Altman, Howard B., and Robert L. Politzer (eds.), 1971. *Individualizing Foreign Language Instruction: The Proceedings of the Stanford Conference.* Rowley (Mass.): Newbury House.

Andersson, Theodore, 1969. *Foreign Languages in the Elementary School: A Struggle Against Mediocrity.* Austin: University of Texas Press.

Bigge, Morris L., 1971. *Learning Theories for Teachers* (Second Ed.) New York: Harper & Row.

Brooks, Nelson, 1964. *Language and Language Learning: Theory and Practice* (Second Ed.) New York: Harcourt Brace Jovanovich.

–––, 1972. *The Audiolingual Reform in Language Learning.* New York: Harcourt Brace Jovanovich.

Chastain, Kenneth, 1971. *The Development of Modern Language Skills: Theory to Practice.* Language and the Teacher: A Series in Applied Linguistics, Vol. 14. Philadelphia: The Center for Curriculum Development, Inc. (CCD books are now sold by Rand McNally, Chicago.)

Cornfield, Ruth, 1966. *Foreign Language Instruction: Dimensions and Horizons.* New York: Appleton-Century-Crofts.

Dacanay, Fe R., 1963. *Techniques and Procedures in Second Language Teaching.* Philippine Center for Language Study Monograph Series, Number 3, Dobbs Ferry (N.Y.): Oceana Publications, Inc.

Diller, Karl Conrad, 1971. *Generative Grammar, Structural Linguistics, and Language Teaching.* Rowley (Mass.): Newbury House.

Disick, Renée S., 1975. *Individualizing Language Instruction: Strategies and Methods.* New York: Harcourt Brace Jovanovich.

Dodson, C. J., 1967. *Language Teaching and the Bilingual Method.* London: Sir Isaac Pitman and Sons, Ltd.

Donoghue, Mildred R., 1967. *Foreign Languages and the Schools: A Book of Readings.* Dubuque (Iowa); William C. Brown.

———, 1968. *Foreign Languages and the Elementary School Child.* Dubuque (Iowa): William C. Brown.

Dorry, Gertrude Nye, 1966. *Games for Second Language Learning.* New York: McGraw-Hill.

Ebel, Robert L., Victor H. Noll, and Roger M. Bauer (eds.), 1969. *Encyclopedia of Educational Research* (Fourth Ed.) New York: Macmillan.

Etmekjian, James, 1966. *Pattern Drills in Language Teaching.* New York: New York University Press.

Farb, Peter, 1974. *Word Play: What Happens When People Talk.* New York: Alfred A. Knopf.

Finocchiario, Mary and Michael Bonomo, 1973. *The Foreign Language Learner: A Guide for Teachers.* New York: Regents.

Grittner, Frank M., 1969. *Teaching Foreign Languages.* New York: Harper & Row.

Grittner, Frank M. (ed.), 1974a. *Student Motivation and the Foreign Language Teacher.* Skokie (Ill.): National Textbook Co.

———, 1974b. *Careers, Communication Culture.* Skokie (Ill.): National Textbook Co.

Grittner, Frank M., and Fred La Leike, 1973. *Individualized Foreign Language Instruction.* Skokie (Ill.): National Textbook Co.

Hall, Edward T., 1959. *The Silent Language.* New York: Fawcett World Library.

Hamilton, Stanley, 1973. "Rural/Urban Interpenetration in Peasant France: A Social Science Approach for French Teachers." Unpublished doctoral dissertation, University of Michigan.

Hester, Ralph (ed.), 1970. *Teaching a Living Language.* New York: Harper & Row.

Hocking, Elton, 1967. *Language Laboratory and Language Learning* (Second Ed.) Washington: Department of Audiovisual Instruction (now Association for Educational Communications and Technology, NEA).

Huebener, Theodore, 1959. *How to Teach Foreign Languages Effectively.* New York: New York University Press.

———, 1960. *Audio-Visual Techniques in Teaching Foreign Languages.* New York: New York University Press.

———, 1961. *Why Johnny Should Learn Foreign Languages.* Philadelphia: Chilton Co.

Jakobovits, Leon, 1970. *Foreign Language Learning: A Psycholinguistic Analysis of the Issues.* Rowley (Mass.): Newbury House.

Kadler, Eric H., 1970. *Linguistics and Teaching Foreign Languages.* New York: Van Nostrand Reinhold.

Kelly, L. G., 1969. *25 Centuries of Language Teaching.* Rowley (Mass.): Newbury House.

Lado, Robert, 1961. *Language Testing: The Construction and Use of Foreign Language Tests.* New York: McGraw-Hill.

———, 1964. *Language Teaching: A Scientific Approach.* New York: McGraw-Hill.

Levenson, Stanley, and William Kendrick (eds.), 1967. *Readings in Foreign Languages for the Elementary School.* Waltham (Mass.): Blaisdell Publishing Co.

Libbish, B. (ed.), 1964. *Advances in the Teaching of Modern Languages,* Vol. I. New York: Macmillan.

Logan, Gerald E., 1973. *Individualized Foreign Language Learning: An Organic Process.* Rowley (Mass.): Newbury House.

Love, F. William D., and Lucille J. Honig, 1973. *Options and Perspectives: A Sourcebook of Innovative Foreign Language Programs in Action, K-12.* New York: Modern Language Association of America.

Mackey, William Francis, 1965. *Language Teaching Analysis.* Bloomington (Ind.): Indiana University Press.

Mathieu, G. (ed.), 1966. *Advances in the Teaching of Modern Languages,* Vol. II. Oxford: Pergamon Press.

Méras, Edmond A., 1962. *A Language Teacher's Guide* (Second Ed.) New York: Harper & Row.

Michel, Joseph (ed.), 1967. *Foreign Language Teaching: An Anthology.* New York: Macmillan.

Moulton, Wm. G., 1970. *Linguistic Guide to Language Learning* (Second Ed.) New York: Modern Language Association.

Nostrand, Howard Lee, David William Foster, and Clay Benjamin Christensen, 1965. *Bibliography of Research on Language Teaching 1945-1964.* Seattle: University of Washington.

Nostrand, Howard Lee. "Empathy for a second culture: motivations and techniques," in (Gilbert Jarvis, ed.) *ACTFL Review of Foreign Language Education.* Vol. 5. Skokie (Ill.): National Textbook Company. 263-327.

Oliva, Peter F., 1969. *The Teaching of Foreign Languages.* Englewood Cliffs (N.J.): Prentice Hall.

Ornstein, Jacob and William W. Gage, 1964. *The ABC's of Languages and Linguistics.* Philadelphia: Chilton Books.

Pei, Mario, 1965. *The Story of Language* (Rev. Ed.) New York: New American Library, Mentor.

Pillet, Roger A., 1974. *Foreign-Language Study: Perspective and Prospect.* Chicago: University of Chicago Press.

Pimsleur, Paul and Terence Quinn, 1971. *The Psychology of Second Language Learning.* Papers from the Second International Congress of Applied Linguistics, Cambridge, 1969. Cambridge (England): Cambridge University Press.

Politzer, Robert L., 1965. *Teaching French: An Introduction to Applied Linguistics.* Boston (Mass.): Ginn.

–––, 1968. *Teaching German: A Linguistic Orientation.* Waltham (Mass.): Blaisdell.

–––, 1970. *Foreign Language Learning.* Englewood Cliffs (N.J.): Prentice Hall.

Politzer, Robert L., and Frieda N. Politzer, 1972. *Teaching English as a Second Language.* Lexington (Mass.): Xerox.

Politzer, Robert L., and Charles N. Staubach, 1965. *Teaching Spanish: A Linguistic Orientation.* Waltham (Mass.): Blaisdell.

Rivers, Wilga M., 1964. *The Psychologist and the Language Teacher.* Chicago: University of Chicago Press.

–––, 1968. *Teaching Foreign-Language Skills.* Chicago: University of Chicago Press.

–––, 1972. *Speaking in Many Tongues.* Rowley (Mass.): Newbury House.

–––, 1975. *A Practical Guide to the Teaching of French.* New York: Oxford University Press.

Rivers, Wilga M., Katherine Mitchell Dell'Orto, and Vincent Dell'Orto, 1975. *A Practical Guide to the Teaching of German.* New York: Oxford University Press.

Rivers, Wilga M., et al., 1976. *A Practical Guide to the Teaching of Spanish.* New York: Oxford University Press.

Smith, George E., and M. Phillip Leamon, 1972. *Effective Foreign Language Instruction in the Secondary School.* Englewood Cliffs (N.J.): Prentice Hall.

Stack, Edward M., 1971. *The Language Laboratory and Modern Language Learning* (Third Ed.) London: Oxford University Press.

Stanislawczyk, Irene E. and Symond Yavener, 1976. *Creativity in the Language Classroom.* Rowley (Mass.): Newbury House.

Steiner, Florence, 1975. *Performing with Objectives.* Rowley (Mass.): Newbury House.

Stevick, Earl W., 1971. *Adapting and Writing Language Lessons.* Washington, D.C.: Dept. of State, Foreign Service Institute. (Superintendent of Documents Stock Number 4400-1365.)

Thomas, Owen, 1965. *Transformational Grammar and the Teacher of English.* New York: Holt Rinehart and Winston.

Travers, Robert M. W. (ed.), 1973. *Second Handbook of Research on Teaching.* Chicago: Rand McNally.

Valdman, Albert (ed.), 1966. *Trends in Language Teaching.* New York: McGraw-Hill.
Valette, Rebecca M., 1967. *Modern Language Testing: A Handbook.* New York: Harcourt Brace Jovanovich.
Valette, Rebecca M., and Renée S. Disick, 1972. *Modern Language Performance Objectives and Individualization: A Handbook.* New York: Harcourt Brace Jovanovich.

Index

Hebeisen, Ardyth 119
Hester, Ralph 101, 123, 125
*Hispania* 92, 111
History of language teaching 100
Hocking, Elton 103, 122, 125
Honig, Lucille J. 50, 102, 125
Howe, Leland W. 50, 119, 120
Howe, Mary Martha 119
Huberman, Gisela 6, 115
Huebener, Theodore 102, 125

Individualized instruction 63-71, 84
    checklist for observation of 70
    definitions of 64-65
Instructional Objectives Exchange 115
Interaction analysis 104
*Instructor, The* 111
*International Review of Applied*
    *Linguistics* (IRAL) 112

Jack, William 115
Jakobovits, Leon 100, 116, 125
James, Muriel 119
Jarvis, Gilbert A. 5, 10, 116, 120
Jay, Charles 118
Jenks, Frederick L. 35
Jian, Gerard 123
Johnson, David W. 120
Joiner, Elizabeth 19, 117
Jongeward, Dorothy 119
Juaire O.F.M., Dennis 44

Kadler, Eric H. 101, 125
Kalivoda, Theodore B. 8, 43, 115, 116,
    123
Kapfer, Philip G. 69, 122
Keating, Marianne 50, 120
Kelly, L. G. 92, 100, 125
Kendrick, William 102, 125
Kinesics 118
Kirschenbaum, Howard 50, 119
Krupar, Karen R. 120

Lado, Robert 27, 103, 125
Ladu, Tora Tuve 27
Lafayette Robert C. 103, 119
LaLeike, Fred 102
Lambert, W. E. 67, 121
*Language and Language Behavior*
    *Abstracts* (LLBA) 112
*Language Learning* 112
Language learning theories 100-101

*Language Teaching and Linguistics:*
    *Abstract* 112
LAP 69
Leamon, M. Phillip 126
*Learning: The Magazine for Creative*
    *Teaching* 112
Lee, Alben 105
Lenard, Yvonne 123
Lenneberg, Eric H. 16, 117
Levenson, Stanley 102, 125
Libbish, B. 125
Listening skills 6-8
Lock, Joan Tuskes 50, 120
Logan, Gerald E. 64-65, 68, 69, 70, 102,
    122, 125
Lohnes, Walter 116
Love, F. William D. 50, 67, 102, 120,
    122, 125
Lowry, William H. 18
Lyon, Harold C., Jr. 120

Mackey, William Francis 101, 125
Maslow, Abraham 49, 120
Mathieu, G. 125
McIntyre, James 119
McKay, Llewelyn R. 16
McKim, Lester W. 69, 122
Meade, Betsy 39
Medish, Vadim 6
Meiden, Walter 123
Méras, Edmond 100, 125
Michel, Joseph 10, 116, 125
Modern Greek Studies Association 108
Modern Language Association 108
*Modern Language Journal, The* 112-113
Morain, Genelle 8, 39, 43, 115, 116, 118, 119
Morel, Stefano 50, 120
Morrey, Robert A. 68, 122
Moskowitz, Gertrude 67, 104, 105, 106,
    122
Moulton, Wm. G. 100, 126
Mueller, Klaus A. 104, 106
Mueller, Theodore 5, 69, 116
Muñoz, Olivia 45
Murdock, George P. 27

National Association of Educational
    Broadcasters 104, 106
National Association of Language
    Laboratory Directors 109
*National Society for the Study of*
    *Education Yearbook* 113
Nelson, Robert J. 67, 122